W9-BCO-316

# BARRON'S

# HOME FARM HANDBOOK

## PETER FORD

First edition for the United States,
Canada, and the Philippine
Republic published by Barron's
Educational Series, Inc., 2000.

Originally published in English by
HarperCollins*Publishers* Ltd under
the title: **COLLINS HOME FARM
HANDBOOK**

© HarperCollins*Publishers*

Peter Ford asserts the moral right
to be identified as the Author of
this work.

*All inquiries should be addressed to:*
Barron's Educational Series, Inc.
250 Wireless Boulevard
Hauppauge, New York 11788
**http://www.barronseduc.com**

Library of Congress Catalog Card
No. 99-068791

International Standard Book No.
0-7641-5212-2

This book was created by
**SP Creative Design**
Editor: Heather Thomas
Art Director: Rolando Ugolini

Photography: Charlie Colmer

Color origination by
Colourscan, Singapore
Printed in Hong Kong

# Contents

# Introduction

Looking after livestock on a warm summer's day can be idyllic but it can also be the last straw during a January hailstorm. Bees don't need a baby-sitter but poultry and goats will need tucking in at night. So before you decide to keep any livestock, you should examine your lifestyle and the amount of time you are prepared to commit to their management. You are embarking on a unique relationship that may last several years and it's important to make the right choice. Assess your own skills and the time and labor you are prepared to put into sustaining that relationship.

Examine your motive for stocking up on honey, eggs, or milk. Why are you contemplating keeping poultry or waterfowl? There is a certain romance to the sight and sound of the honeybee foraging for nectar high in the dappled foliage and blossom of a sun-drenched orchard but do you really want to put your hand in the hive to steal the fruits of her labor?

No one says you have to fall in love with your animals but you will at least need to develop a nodding acquaintance with the signs of healthy appetite and behavior. A good standard of stockmanship is built up over time and alarm bells will ring when your goat doesn't greet you in her usual way.

Some people have a knack with poultry and just seem to know instinctively what to do when something seems amiss. But for the rest of us it is a comfort to know that every duckling or chick has the will to live and so long as we provide the means to health, mortalities will prove exceptional events and not the imagined rule of our nightmares. Confidence increases with time and you will be amazed how quickly you will learn to care for your animals. You can derive great pleasure from keeping farm animals and you will have the satisfaction of knowing that they have a pleasant life, too.

**Peter Ford**

# CHAPTER ONE

# Keeping Chickens

Developing and managing a small flock of chickens for the production of eggs is one of the commonest forms of livestock management undertaken by the amateur or hobbyist. This backyard or home flock can be kept very simple or made more complex, depending on the aims of the poultry keeper. There is obviously a point at which an amateur keeper can suddenly find that his hobby is taking up more and more of his time.

# Introduction

Hens will produce fertile eggs if run with a rooster and so, if a limit is to be placed on flock size, cock birds should be excluded. It is better for a complete novice to keep a flock of chickens on a small scale at the outset, allowing time for familiarization and gaining experience of poultry keeping before attempting to expand. The scale of the operation can be increased gradually over time and it is wiser to grow into the job rather than overstretch your resources unduly at the beginning.

## TERMINOLOGY

The term fowl is usually restricted to the common domestic chicken, *Gallus gallus*. In poultry parlance, fowl commonly means a fully grown female bird.
- Young birds of both sexes are called *chickens*.
- Male chickens are called roosters or *cocks*.
- Females, especially those more than a year old, are called *hens*.
- Females less than a year old are called *pullets*.
- Very young chickens of either sex are called *chicks*.
- Castrated males are called *capons*.

## HISTORY AND ORIGINS

Chickens and their produce are such an integral part of our daily lives that it is hard to think of a more ubiquitous creature. From their beginnings in Southwest Asia, they have spread to every corner of the world due in part to their usefulness to man. Charles Darwin considered them descendants of a single wild species, the red jungle fowl, *G. gallus*, which is found in the wild state from India through Southeast Asia to the Philippines.

The chicken was one of the first domestic animals to be mentioned in recorded history; it is referred to in ancient Chinese documents that indicate that this creature of the west was introduced into China about 1400 B.C. Fowl are depicted in Babylonian carvings of about 600 B.C. and are mentioned by early Greek writers, notably by the playwright Aristophanes, about 400 B.C. The Romans considered chickens to be sacred to Mars, their god of war.

## ANATOMY

Like the turkey, pheasant, quail, and other members of the order Galliformes, chickens are adapted for living on the ground, where they find their natural foods, consisting chiefly of worms, insects, seeds, and greenstuff. Their feet, usually four-toed, except in the English Dorking breed, are designed specifically for scratching the earth.

The large, heavy body and short wings make most breeds incapable of flying except for short distances. The crop is large and the gizzard strongly muscular. In adults of both sexes the head is decorated with wattles and with a naked, fleshy crest, called the comb, which is more prominent in the male and is variously shaped in the different breeds and varieties. The typical comb is single, serrated, and relatively large, either erect or drooping.

### Size and shape

In size and shape, the various breeds show great diversity. The 12-lb (5-kg) Brahma cock, for example, has a miniature counterpart, the Bantam, weighing only about 20 oz (about 567 g). The proportions of the long-legged game fowl contrast sharply with those of the squat Cochin.

The stubby tail of the latter is one extreme. However, another extreme is presented by the Japanese or Yokohama breed, in which the tail feathers of the cock may be as long as 6 ft (2 m). In general, the members of one breed are alike in shape, the varieties of the breed differing only in minor characteristics, such as the shape of the comb, and in color and markings.

**Right:** *The head is decorated with wattles and a fleshy comb, which may be single or serrated, erect or drooping.*

## HABITS AND CHARACTERISTICS

In habit, chickens are strictly diurnal, highly gregarious, and polygamous. Cocks of the game breeds are especially noted for their courage and pugnacity.

Unless otherwise trained, female chickens lay their eggs on the ground, in tall grass or weeds. Periodically, domestic hens become broody; that is, they stop laying and show a strong desire to sit on their nests and hatch chicks.

The incubation period for the eggs is approximately three weeks. The chicks, when hatched, are covered with down and can run around immediately. Although they are able to feed themselves, newly hatched chicks can survive for about a week without eating, subsisting on the egg yolk that is included in the abdomen.

## Breeds and varieties

Numerous breeds and several hundred varieties of fowl are now recognized. New varieties are in the making, moreover, as breeders strive to improve their stock for particular purposes. The breeds may be classified according to the parts of the world in which they originated and also according to their function.

**Below:** *The Chamois Poland male has a distinctive crest of feathers.*

### Game fowl and ornamental breeds

Unfortunately these are still bred in some areas for their fighting qualities. Elsewhere, game breeds are now kept by fanciers for ornamental purposes and for exhibition at poultry shows. The exhibition varieties of game fowl are characterized by their long necks and shanks and sparse tail feathers. Other ornamental breeds include the Bantam, the Japanese fowl, the Polish fowl with its great crest of feathers, the downy-feathered Silkie, and the ragged-looking Frizzle.

## ECONOMICALLY IMPORTANT BREEDS

Among breeds of economic importance, the oldest class, originating in China in the remote past, is the Asian group, which includes the Brahma, the Cochin, and Langshan. They are large, heavy birds with thick, fluffy plumage and feathered shanks. Their meat is coarse in texture but they can be poor egg producers. They are hardy, however, and thrive in cold climates. Asian stock has contributed greatly to the formation of the modern American breeds.

English fowl are distinguished for the fine quality of their meat and, like the French breeds, are more valuable as table birds than as egg layers. However, the Light Sussex are good layers, as are the Dorkings and Orpingtons.

The outstanding egg producers are the Mediterranean breeds, which include the Ancona, Andalusian, Minorca, and the Leghorn. Except for the Minorcas, the Mediterranean fowl tend to be small and are therefore uneconomical as meat poultry, but they consume relatively little feed. They are generally prolific and their white eggs are large in proportion to their body size. The pullets begin to lay early and have poorly developed maternal qualities. Therefore little laying time is lost in broodiness. Being sensitive to environmental changes, these birds are at their healthiest and lay most eggs in mild climates.

## AMERICAN BREEDS

The American class consists of general-purpose breeds developed in the past century to serve as producers of both meat and eggs. American breeds are moderate or large in size, with meat of good quality. They are very hardy and lay well in winter. Rhode Island Reds are often as prolific as single-comb White Leghorns. The maternal instinct is strong in American fowl but in some strains it has been minimized by selective breeding. Usually birds of this class mature later than Mediterranean fowl but earlier than Asian fowl. An exception in this respect is the fast-growing New Hampshire breed.

**Above:** *The light Brahma has a white body with a black tail and black striped neck hackles. It is often kept for showing.*

# What do I want?

Which type of chicken to keep and where to find a reliable supply will depend on the answer to the following question: what comes first in importance, the chicken or the egg? Hybrid chickens are the result of painstaking genetic selection and, as such, are hard to beat for quantity and quality of eggs produced. Traditional purebreds are perhaps more interesting and colorful characters, so if the chicken is more important than the uniformity and number of eggs laid, then purebreds are to be preferred.

**Above:** *Eggs vary greatly in their size and color. They may be brown, white, or speckled.*

## GOOD FREE-RANGE LAYERS

There is not a lot to choose from between hybrid commercial layers because they have all been well-engineered for the job, but there is a difference between using a type bred for free-range conditions and ones bred for indoor systems. The range-type layer is the best of the hybrid bunch for home-producers. It is marginally heavier than chickens bred for intensive conditions, and hardier, too. They include the Lohmann Brown, Bovans Nera, Black Rock and Hisex Ranger. The pick of the traditional pure breeds, delivering a reasonable number of eggs, includes the Rhode Island Red, Wyandotte, Leghorn, and Light Sussex.

### Egg appearance
The appearance of the egg itself is a matter of personal taste. Some people like the look of a brown egg whereas others plump for white. There is no nutritional evidence to suggest that one is better than the other but egg color will usually have a bearing on breed selection.

A hen will always lay the same color egg, regardless of the rooster with whom she mates. Egg color is accounted for by pigments in the eggshell. White eggs simply indicate a lack of pigment. Brown pigment is actually deposited on the surface of the shell.

## BUYING CHICKENS

Although chickens are a very common sight, birds are not usually available off the shelf. The main reason for this is that no one really wants to raise pullets without having a ready market for them. Commercial birds are raised and sold under contract and growers do not usually sell small numbers to casual callers. Purebreds are equally hard to source for the same reasons but with the added difficulty of rarity; there are just fewer of them.

This is not to imply that a preferred breed will be impossible to find but if a particular strain is as rare as hen's teeth, then there may well be a very good reason for this; namely, that the local conditions are unfavorable for the breed. Researching the resident poultry population will provide you with useful information. If most people are keeping Rhode Island Reds, there must be a good case for following suit.

Another important question to be decided concerns age. At what stage in the poultry life cycle will the flock be started? Is it to begin with fertile eggs ready for the incubator or is it to kick off with point-of-lay pullets?

For the sake of simplicity, adult birds are a much easier option but the sense of satisfaction is that much greater if a flock is established from scratch. As a rule, it is not as hard to find point-of-lay pullets as it is to buy fertile eggs.

Ask around in your area to find a reputable poultry breeder who has good, healthy stock. Don't be tempted to buy chickens at market if you don't know where they have come from or if they don't look really healthy and in good condition. Go to a breeder instead. Other sources you can go to include 4-H and livestock shows.

### Number of eggs

The exact number of eggs any particular breed will lay is a hotly disputed topic but some breeds are renowned for high levels of production. There is obviously a need to compromise on some aspect of the ideal. One breed may please the eye, be broody, hardy, and docile but may lay the wrong colored egg for your taste.

A hybrid can lay over 300 eggs a year while other more traditional strains can produce only half this number. Three or four hybrid birds will produce ample eggs for the average family's needs. The first two years are the best. Hens often stop laying while in moult and resume when they are refeathered. They may also stop laying through the winter months unless they are given some artificial light to extend the daylight hours.

The life expectancy of a hen has been known to extend to ten years, and thus the decision on breed selection could be difficult to change in the short term.

# Who's who in the hen house

## DORKING

### Origin
The Dorking is believed to have originated in Italy, having been introduced into Great Britain by the Romans. Much of its development took place in England from where it has gained worldwide popularity.

### Characteristics
The Dorking has a rectangular body set on very short legs. It is five-toed and has a relatively large comb. They are good layers, will go broody, and make good mothers but they need shelter in very cold weather.

**Above:** *Silver Grey Dorking cockerel*

## FACT FILE

**VARIETIES:**
- White
- Silver Grey
- Colored

**STANDARD WEIGHTS:**
- **Cock:** 7–9 lb (3–4 kg)
- **Hen:** 6–7 lb (2.7–3 kg)
- **Pullet:** 5–6 lb (2.2–2.7 kg)

**SKIN COLOR:**
- White

**EGGSHELL COLOR:**
- White

**USE**
A good general-purpose fowl that, although developed mainly as a table bird, provides ample egg production.

# LEGHORN

## Origin
Leghorns take their name from Livorno, the Italian city where they originated, but most of their development has occurred since their introduction to North America, where they are most numerous.

## Characteristics
Small and noisy, Leghorns are quick on their feet and good foragers. They are flighty and, although noted as egg producers, rarely go broody.

**Above:** *Chequered Leghorn*

# PLYMOUTH ROCK

### Origin

The invention of this bird is contested by several individuals but there is no disputing its North American nationality. The first Plymouth Rock was barred and proved exceptionally popular with breeders and keepers.

### Characteristics

Plymouth Rocks are a good general farmyard fowl. They are docile and will normally go broody. They usually make good mothers and possess a long, broad back, a moderately deep, full breast and an upright single comb of medium size. They produce about 200 eggs per year and are long-lived.

**Above:** *Barred Plymouth Rock*

## FACT FILE

**VARIETIES:**
■ Barred

■ White

■ Buff

■ Partridge

■ Silver Pencilled

■ Blue

■ Columbian

**STANDARD WEIGHTS:**
■ **Cock:** 9 lb (4 kg)

■ **Hen:** 7–8 lb (3–3.5 kg)

■ **Pullet:** 6 lb (2.7 kg)

**SKIN COLOR:**
■ Yellow

**EGGSHELL COLOR:**
■ Light brown

**USE**
Attractive fowl that is a good egg producer. Hardy and vigorous.

# RHODE ISLAND RED

## FACT FILE

**VARIETIES:**
- Single comb
- Rose comb

**STANDARD WEIGHTS:**
- **Cock:** 8–9 lb (3.5–4 kg)
- **Hen:** 6–7 lb (2.7–3 kg)
- **Pullet:** 5–6 lb (2.2–2.7 kg)

**SKIN COLOR:**
- Yellow

**EGGSHELL COLOR:**
- Brown

**USE**
Fine dual-purpose medium to heavy chicken with a good rate of lay.

### Origin

Developed in the New England area around Rhode Island and Massachusetts, the Rhode Island Red has a strong Malay bloodline and has the resultant deep color and strong constitution.

### Characteristics

This breed is a good choice for the small flock keeper because they are hardy and very good layers. They can cope with marginal diets and poor housing while still continuing to produce eggs. They are one of the few breeds where exhibition qualities and production ability sit together in a single strain.

**Above:** *Rhode Island Red male*

15

# WYANDOTTE

## Origin
This breed has its roots in North America at the end of the nineteenth century. The Silver Laced variety was developed in New York State and the other strains of Wyandotte followed from breeders in other northern and northeastern states.

## Characteristics
These birds are a good choice for small free-ranging flocks kept under rugged conditions and they will go broody and make good mothers. They are attractive, with a good temperament and a fine variety of colors, making them of interest to fanciers as well as egg producers.

## FACT FILE

**VARIETIES:**
- White
- Buff
- Columbian
- Golden Laced, Silver Laced
- Blue
- Partridge
- Black
- Silver-Pencilled

**STANDARD WEIGHTS:**
- **Cock:** 8–9 lb (3.5–4 kg)
- **Hen:** 6–7 lb (2.7–3 kg)
- **Pullet:** 5–6 lb (2.2–2.7 kg)

**SKIN COLOR:**
- Yellow

**EGGSHELL COLOR:**
- Brown

**USE**
Dual-purpose breed with good laying ability.

**Above:** *Silver Pencilled Wyandotte*

# AUSTRALORP

## FACT FILE

**VARIETIES:**
- Black
- Blue

**STANDARD WEIGHTS:**
- **Cock:** 8–9 lb (3.5–4 kg)
- **Hen:** 6–7 lb (2.7–3 kg)
- **Pullet:** 5–6 lb (2.2–2.7 kg)

**SKIN COLOR:**
- White

**EGGSHELL COLOR:**
- Mid-brown

**USE**
A very good egg producer of intermediate body size.

### Origin
As the name implies, this breed is an Australian development of the Orpington. Developed from Black Orpington stock, it is smaller with a trimmer figure than its heavier English ancestor.

### Characteristics
Australorps have an intense beetle-green sheen to their black plumage and are one of the best dual-purpose chickens. They have no special requirements and enjoy a dustbath in dry soil or sand.

**Above:** *Australorp Blue Bantam*

# COCHIN

### Origin
This breed started out in China but later underwent considerable development in North America and is now a widespread ornamental fowl.

### Characteristics
Cochins are fluffy balls of feathers and are kept for their beauty rather than their utility. They are very broody and make excellent foster mothers but they do not lay many eggs (about 100 per year).

**Above:** *Buff Cochins*

## FACT FILE

**VARIETIES:**
■ Black

■ Buff

■ Partridge

■ White

**STANDARD WEIGHTS:**
■ **Cock:** 11 lb (5 kg)

■ **Hen:** 8–9 lb (3.5–4 kg)

■ **Pullet:** 7 lb (3 kg)

**SKIN COLOR:**
■ Yellow

**EGGSHELL COLOR:**
■ Brown

**USE**
This breed is mainly kept for its looks and for its strong motherly instincts but it is a reasonable layer.

# ORPINGTON

## FACT FILE

**VARIETIES:**
- Black
- Blue
- Buff
- White

**STANDARD WEIGHTS:**
- **Cock:** 10 lb (4.5 kg)
- **Hen:** 8 lb (3.5 kg)
- **Pullet:** 7 lb (3 kg)

**SKIN COLOR:**
- White

**EGGSHELL COLOR:**
- Brown

**USE**
A heavy dual-purpose chicken with good laying ability.

### Origin
Developed in Orpington, Kent, during the 1880s, the breed made early and rapid progress, spreading quickly across the Atlantic to North America.

### Characteristics
This breed appears bigger than it is because of the loose nature of the feathering, which allows it to endure the cold better than some breeds. They are at home in a free-range regime and go broody and make excellent mothers. They are perhaps a little too docile for their own good as they will often lose out in any pecking order when mixing in a flock with other breeds.

**Above:** *Black Orpington Bantam*

# SUSSEX

## Origin

As the name implies, these birds originated in the
English county of Sussex where they were prized as a
table fowl more than 100 years ago. They continue to be
a popular farmyard fowl and the light variety has figured
prominently in the development of many commercial
hybrids. The Sussex is one of the oldest breeds still kept
in relatively large numbers.

## Characteristics

Sussex are alert, attractive and good foragers. They have
rectangular bodies; the speckled variety is especially
pleasing on the eye with its multicolored plumage. They
go broody and make good mothers. The Sussex provides
a happy combination of both exhibition and utility
features. They are extremely good layers.

**Above:** *Light Sussex*

### FACT FILE

**VARIETIES:**
- Speckled
- Red
- Light

**STANDARD WEIGHTS:**
- **Cock:** 9 lb (4 kg)
- **Hen:** 7 lb (3 kg)
- **Pullet:** 6 lb (2.7 kg)

**SKIN COLOR:**
- White

**EGGSHELL COLOR:**
- Brown

**USE**
- A good general-purpose breed for producing eggs.

# What do they need?

Healthy, happy chickens need a warm, dry, and secure hen house to protect them from adverse weather and drafts, keep them safe from predators, provide the hens with privacy when laying their eggs, and give them a roost for the night.

## HOUSING

The type and size of housing will be determined by your aims and the size of the flock. If your objective is to run half-a-dozen purebred chickens for the fun of it, then the hen house can be simple, relatively small, and unsophisticated. There are, however, basic requirements to be met whatever the scale.

There are countless coop designs but most common garden sheds or existing buildings can be adapted to accommodate chickens. The simplest, cheapest, and most natural way to keep poultry is free-range. Regardless of the specifics of design, there are four general points that you should bear in mind when housing poultry:
■ Security     ■ Space
■ Weatherproofing ■ Cleanliness.

### Security
It is surprising how many poultry-keepers lose flocks to predators. Most attacks occur at night and are carried out by foxes, mice, rats, and dogs. Protection is always the best form of prevention so buy or build a hen

house with security in mind from the start. Role playing can be useful, so try thinking like a hungry fox or dog when considering the design of the hen house. You may need to provide the following:
■ A secure fence around the birds' enclosure, with its base buried in the ground to stop animals burrowing underneath. It can also help shelter birds from strong winds and provide welcome shade in hot sunshine.
■ Security lights that are triggered by movement.
■ A secure door for shutting the hens in at night. Never forget to do this.

**Above:** *A tall fence with the base buried in the ground will protect your hens from predators.*

## Space

Adequate floor space is essential. At least 1 sq ft (30 sq cm) per hen is needed or 8 sq in (20 sq cm) for bantams. Don't make the hen house too small – the more space you can provide the better.

## Weatherproofing

The hen house should provide adequate shelter for your birds, protecting them against the wind and against extremes of heat and cold. Houses may be movable or static, both of which have their own specific advantages and disadvantages. Although movable houses and pens enable you to provide fresh ground for the hens, they will not last as long as a brick or stone building. If the hen house is static, you may have to provide a wind shelter parallel to the pophole entry to prevent wind from entering the house. Likewise, if the hens have an outside run, building a windbreak of board or corrugated tin around the bottom of the fence will help to protect the birds.

Most hen houses are made of timber with wooden or plyboard siding. A sloping roof will enable the rain to run off, but do not use felt as this can encourage mites.

**Above:** *You can buy custom-made wooden hen houses, with removable walls and doors for easy access and cleaning. They can be moved around and placed in a wired or fenced enclosure, if wished.*

**Right:** *Hen houses can be raised above the ground to help protect the chickens against small predators.*

**Above:** *More elaborate hen houses with an adjoining run and outside nesting boxes can be made. On this attractive Shaker-style hen house, the roofs lift up and the doors can be removed.*

**Left:** *These more traditional designs made of wood with a protected run have the advantage that the chickens can go outside or inside at will. The sloping roofs enable the rain to run off easily. They can also be moved around easily preventing the formation of muddy patches.*

## Cleanliness

Keeping the hen house clean and removing droppings and soiled litter are very important if you are to keep your birds healthy and free of disease. You must clean it at least once a week and replace all the litter. Make sure that the disinfectant you use is not toxic. You can buy specially formulated products that destroy harmful bacteria.

## Lighting

The amount of light available will influence the egg production. Natural daylight reaches a maximum during June and then begins to decrease. Artificial lights controlled with a time clock are used by some people to hold the light-day constant. They use either morning and evening lights, or both, to lengthen the light-day. The cost of lighting a layer house is very low and will result in higher egg production during the winter months. If you do decide to give your hens extra lighting in this way, you must continue doing so until March or April when the amount of light lengthens considerably. Otherwise, you risk confusing the hens and this may affect their breeding season.

For extra light in the hen house, you can provide windows near the roof. A sliding cover is safer than glass.

## Insulation

Insulation is any material that reduces the rate at which heat is transferred from inside the house to the outside or vice versa. All

**Above:** *Inside the hen house, some good-quality straw or wood shavings should be strewn across the floor and in the nest boxes.*

building materials have some insulation value. Normal construction materials such as wood or tin do not provide enough insulation, however, and should be supplemented with more effective insulating materials. If a non-edible insulation is used, it must be protected so that the chickens can't access it.

Insulation conserves heat during brooding and reduces the rate of heat build-up in hot weather. An insulated building is cooler in the warm part of the afternoon and warmer in the cold early morning hours. In addition, surface condensation (sweating) can be controlled in an insulated building.

## Ventilation

Correct ventilation of the hen house is of major importance if birds are housed for long periods. The purpose of ventilation is to remove any moisture from inside the building and to prevent condensation, remove excess heat in hot weather, remove gases from droppings, and provide fresh air for the chickens.

The least expensive system to use is natural ventilation. Windows or panels located in the top one-half of the wall that lean back inside at the top and latch at different angles and that can also be raised from the bottom or be removed completely, can provide the basis for such a system. This system works best if the windows or panels are located on all four walls of the building. Panels, rather than windows, should be used on the north wall. Low hanging doors can also be used in extremely warm weather.

The prevailing winds, air temperature, age of the birds, moisture, and gaseous conditions all determine how far to open the windows and whether the air flow is directed toward the ceiling or allowed to flow straight in. During cold weather and

**Right:** *For easy egg collection, you can access the nest boxes from the outside of the hen house rather than venturing inside.*

with young birds, drafts at the level of the birds must be avoided.

The house needs to be dry, as close to 70°F (19°C) as possible, and as free from undesirable gases and odors as possible. No amount of ventilation will keep a dirty, dusty, manure-laden hen house comfortable for its occupants.

## Nest boxes

An adequate number of well-constructed nest boxes will result in cleaner eggs and fewer broken ones. Provide an individual nest for every four layers. Nests can be arranged along the walls, preferably in the darkest areas as hens prefer to lay secretly

**Right:** *Always provide water for your chickens, as with these Gold Brahmas.*

should be 16–24 in (40–60 cm) above the floor with 1 x 2 in (2.5 x 5 cm) welded wire below the roost to keep hens out of the droppings.

### Litter

Start with 4 in (10 cm) of a moisture-absorbent litter, such as wood shavings. It is labor saving to have a store of fresh litter ready either in the house or in a store nearby. Keep the litter dry and in a loose, uncaked condition. Wet litter causes dirty eggs and increases the risk of disease. Preventing water spillage and leaks and providing proper ventilation will keep the litter in good condition. Agitate the litter when it becomes damp and packed. Remove any wet spots and replace with fresh litter.

### Feeders

One 4-ft (1.2-m) trough, open on both sides, is enough for twenty-five to thirty layers. Trough feeders can be purchased ready-made or they may be home-made. They should be equipped with a grille to prevent birds treading in them. Suspended tube feeders can be used for up to twenty-five layers. The lip of the feeder should be kept level with the hens' backs. You can buy step-on feeders that keep the food dry and safe from vermin. The hen lifts the lid by stepping on to the step of the trough.

and undisturbed. There should be an easily accessible egg collection point for you on the outside of the hen house. The nests should have perches below the entrance, with the lowest nest being 10–20 in (25–50 cm) above the floor. Line the nest boxes with wood shavings or fresh, clean straw and cover the floor of the hen house with the same litter. Avoid hay which can easily become mouldy and cause breathing problems for the hens.

### Droppings boards

Droppings boards or pits and roosts are optional but they do help to prevent manure build-up in the litter. Roosts are usually placed over a droppings board or pit. Wooden roost poles can be made from 2 x 2-in (5 x 5-cm) pieces with the upper edges slightly rounded. Roosts

## Waterers

Fresh, clean water should be available at all times. This might mean providing a water heater during the winter months or making four or five trips to the hen house each day to remove ice and replenish with fresh water. Waterers should be adjusted to the same height as the feeders. They can be placed on wire platforms about 4–6 in (10–12.5 cm) high to help prevent wet litter and water contamination. Outside water troughs should be moved around regularly to prevent damaged grass and small areas of mud.

**Below:** *The chickens should have access to food and water. Move feeders and waterers frequently to prevent mud patches forming.*

## FEEDING THE HENS

Twenty-five light breed hens in good production will eat 5–7 lb (2–3 kg) of feed per day. The home flock owner will probably get the best results by feeding a complete commercial layer feed that contains fifteen percent protein. All feed should be stored in a covered container to protect it from vermin.

Laying hens should be fed layers' pellets or meal daily. In addition, you can feed about 1 oz (25 g) grain per hen per day, and a range of fresh greens. Although fresh waste products from the kitchen may be used to supplement the hens' regular diet, you must take care over what and how much you offer. Once a day,

feed only what the flock will eat in five to ten minutes. It is very important not to overdo this type of ration and to bear in mind that some kitchen scraps, such as onions and fruit peelings, can cause off-flavor in eggs. Free-range birds will also scratch around for bugs and grubs.

In bad weather, you should feed some grain rather than pellets in the evenings. Make sure that the birds have plenty to eat as this will help them to keep warm in addition to laying eggs.

## BROODING EQUIPMENT

To give day-old chicks a proper start, the brooder must provide a temperature of about 95°F (30°C) in winter and 90°F (28°C) during the rest of the year. Some types of brooders (warm-room, space-type heaters) heat the entire room or house. Others (cool-room) warm the area near

**Right:** *You can keep baby chicks warm by bedding them down in litter, such as wood shavings, on several layers of newspaper under a heat lamp.*

the birds, while the rest of the room remains relatively cool. Cool-room stoves are usually heated with gas or electricity.

In urban areas or when a house that is adequate for brooding is unavailable, an outside electric brooder is simple to construct and relatively inexpensive. Heat for this type of unit is provided by four 40-watt bulbs and is controlled by a thermostat. During cold weather, it might be necessary to increase the size of the bulbs to maintain sufficient heat.

### Gas brooders

Gas brooders with a canopy require little labor, having automated temperature settings, both upward and downward maneuvrability and a low running cost. Disadvantages are moisture condensation

in the house during extremely cold weather and capital expense, if a large capacity storage tank is deemed necessary.

### Electric infrared bulbs

These have a low initial cost, are easy to work under and around, and can be used for supplemental heat with some gas appliances. Disadvantages are that they warm only what they shine on, go off during power failures and do not always provide enough heated areas for cold weather brooding.

### Feeders

Feeder size and length must change with the age of the birds, allowing 1 in (2.5 cm) of feeding space per chick at the outset, using a chick-size feeder filled completely for the first week.

A larger growing feeder (broiler size) is needed when the chicks are about four weeks of age, affording 2 in (5 cm) per bird. The round cylinder hanging feeder can be used as a starting and growing feeder if adjusted correctly.

### Waterers

These also need to change as birds grow. During the first ten to fourteen days, baby chicks are not very big and do not require a lot of water. However, a good supply of clean, fresh water should be available ad lib at all times. Two or three 2-pint (1-liter) jars with fountain bases are sufficient for 100 chicks. After two weeks, these can be replaced by a single 5-gallon

**Above:** *Always make fresh water available to the chicks even though they do not require a lot in the first couple of weeks.*

(22-liter) appliance per 100 chicks or ½ in (1 cm) of automatic trough drinker per chick. At least two appliances are needed for each brood regardless of the number of chicks.

### Brooder guard

A brooder guard should be placed beneath the brooder or heat lamp to keep day-old chicks confined to a warm area. This guard should be circular to stop birds smothering in the corners and will help to prevent drafts. It should be 12 in (30 cm) or more in height and made of material such as hardboard or corrugated cardboard. An additional 10–12 ft (3–4 m) of length is needed for enlarging the circle as birds grow. The guard can be removed when the birds are about ten days old.

# What do I do?

Household poultry flocks may produce a high percentage of dirty eggs. Many of these eggs are soiled because they are laid in dirty nests or on the floor. Dirty eggs can be a health hazard if they are not properly cleaned and sanitized.

## PREVENTING DIRTY EGGS

The best method of control is prevention. Eradicating floor eggs altogether is an impossible task but their number can be minimized if bad habits are discouraged early on. When the pullets are sixteen to eighteen weeks of age, let them have access to nests during the day. Provide at least one nest for four hens. In the evening remove all birds from the nests and close the opening so that the pullets cannot re-enter them for overnight roosting. Nests should be opened again in the early morning. These steps will get the birds into the habit of using nests. Persistent floor layers can be trained by picking them up and putting them on the nest.

Gather eggs at least three times a day. The longer eggs remain in the nest the greater their chances of being broken and

## CLEANING DIRTY EGGS

Even under the best of conditions, some dirty eggs will still be produced. These eggs should be placed in a separate container at collection times to avoid cross-contamination. The dirty eggs can be left to accumulate but must be cleaned at the end of the day. This helps to prevent hardening of the dirt and reduces the chance of microbial penetration of the shell. Follow these directions for cleaning eggs.

■ Dirty eggs should be washed in water that is much warmer than the eggs. A good water temperature is 120°F (40°C) or as hot as the hands can tolerate. This causes the egg contents to expand and prevents the entry of microbe contaminated water through the shell pores.

■ Use a non-foaming, unscented detergent. The fragrance in scented detergents will be absorbed by the eggs, giving them an off-flavor or odor when eaten. Unscented automatic dishwasher or laundry detergent can be used.

■ Home laundry bleach can be used as a sanitizing dip. Prepare the sanitizer according to the manufacturer's directions for a weak disinfectant.

fouling the nest. Gather them twice in the morning and once during mid-to-late afternoon. Nests should be cleaned once a week to remove dirty litter and manure. Replace the soiled nesting material with some clean straw or shavings. Frequent gathering and clean nests are the keys to producing clean eggs.

## NAIL TRIMMING

Chickens' toenails grow constantly and should wear naturally. However, if a bird seems to have excessively long claws, causing a restriction to free and easy movement, trimming is required. Using ordinary nail clippers or dog nail trimmers, trim off the tip or the last quarter of the nail. The blood vessel that feeds the nail can be seen as a reddish line along the center of the nail. Never cut the nail so short that you damage this blood vessel. If you make a mistake and some bleeding occurs, push a cotton swab into the cut surface of the nail and apply pressure until the bleeding stops.

## HANDLING BIRDS

The key to handling poultry lies in the ability to be firm and positive in any action; birds are usually docile but they can peck, scratch or inflict puncture wounds if handled in a tentative fashion. Indeed, roosters may develop large spurs or claws on their legs that can quite easily inflict serious wounds. Most birds will calm down when their heads or eyes are covered by a soft cloth but at the time of capture, the wings must be restrained.

1 With both hands, hold the wings down to the body of the bird.

2 Gather the wings up in one hand nearest the body of the bird.

3 Hold them behind the bird – never make a grab at wing-tips, which can easily break.

4 Restrain the legs between the fingers of the other hand.

Chickens can be caught by the legs if needs be and held upside down for a short period while gaining initial control but this should only be used as a short-term expediency before righting them to the more comfortable handling posture.

**Above:** *When holding a chicken, place your hand underneath, palm spread out upward, with your fingers around the legs.*

# What to expect

## BROODINESS

A hen lays only one egg every day or two. She does not start to incubate them until the whole clutch is laid. This way all the chicks will hatch at the same time. The physiology of a hen changes after her clutch has been laid. She will remain sitting on her eggs with her wings slightly spread to help keep them warm for twenty-one days. She will make muttering, aggressive noises if she is disturbed and may even peck viciously at the cause of any intrusion.

She will only leave the nest once a day to eat, drink and defecate. It is important to make sure the hen does do this at least every other day to avoid the dangers of starvation or getting the eggs

dirty with her droppings. (The broody droppings usually come out in one large, foul-smelling lump.)

Once the chicks start to hatch the hen will remain on the nest with them for twenty-four to twenty-eight hours. Any eggs that have not hatched by then will be left behind when she takes the chicks for their first walk. At this time water and chick feed should be available for the chicks. A hen is also called broody when she is raising her chicks, protecting them, teaching them to find food, and hovering over them to keep them warm.

### Preventing broodiness

Sometimes it may be necessary to prevent a hen hatching her eggs. Putting her in a pen out of sight of her old nest and then keeping her there for four days will usually break up the broodiness. She should, of course, have feed and water. Some stubborn broodies may continue to sit even in a pen without eggs.

## MOULTING

Moulting is the shedding and renewal of feathers and occurs about once a year. The order in which the different sections of

**Left:** *Chickens usually moult once a year and it takes about seven weeks for the new feathers to grow and open up.*

the plumage is shed follows a well-defined pattern, starting at the head and neck and then passing to the body and wings until finally reaching the tail. Moulting is a difficult time for poultry, involving both hormonal fluctuations and increased energy requirements.

### The new feathers

The process of moulting takes about seven weeks to complete its cycle. Immature feathers, called pin or blood feathers, grow through the skin rolled up in a tube-like structure called a keratin sheath. Normally, the bird will use its beak to preen or rub off this sheath, allowing the feather to open up. These immature feathers have a large blood vessel in their center and if the pin feather is torn or damaged, it will bleed excessively. The entire feather in its sheath must be pulled firmly from its attachment to the skin and pressure applied for a few minutes to staunch any bleeding.

## TRANSPORTATION

There are times when you will need to move birds from place to place, either singly or in numbers. Common sense will dictate the specific measures you should adopt, but it is worth noting that poultry can die if not transported properly. The main objective is to minimize the stress brought on by any overcrowding or inadequate ventilation. A covering of some sort is useful but it must allow for

## HYGIENE IN THE HEN HOUSE

1 Provide one nest for each set of four hens.
2 Begin training the pullets to the nest before they start to lay.
3 Clean out the nests once a week.
4 Gather eggs twice in the morning and once in the afternoon.
5 Separate dirty and clean eggs at the time of gathering.
6 Wash dirty eggs in water that is 110–120°F (37–40°C).
7 Do not soak eggs before or during washing.
8 Change the wash water after each three to four dozen eggs cleaned.
9 Rinse each egg in clean water, dip in a sanitizer, and air dry.
10 Keep eggs in a closed container in the refrigerator.

adequate air-flow. Readily available containers include the following:
- Wire cage – solid or wire bottomed.
- Cat carrier – plastic or similar.
- Cardboard box – must be large enough not to restrict movement and have ventilation holes.

It is important to remember to line the floor of any carrier with some kitchen paper or old newspapers to soak up feces and urine and, depending on the duration of the journey, you may have to provide water and food.

# Health issues

Chickens fall foul to many diseases but most health problems can be avoided through good management and diet.

## BACTERIAL PROBLEMS

**Chronic respiratory disease (CRD)**
This is a bacterial infection, characterized by coughing, sneezing, nasal discharge, lethargy and weight loss.

**Infectious coryza** This usually results in swelling of the face around the eyes and wattles. Watery discharge from the eyes results in the lids sticking together. Treat with antibiotics.

## VIRAL DISEASES

**Fowl pox** This results in nodules and scabs on the face, mouth, and throat. It usually lasts for several weeks and proves fatal. Vaccines are available.

**Infectious bronchitis** This is usually characterized by coughing, sneezing, and rattling. The disease usually lasts from ten to fourteen days in a flock. Mortality varies, although chicks are particularly susceptible. Vaccines are available.

**Marek's disease** This usually affects young birds. There are several forms of the disease, which attacks the viscera, the nervous system, the eyes, and the skin. The best means of avoiding it is to source birds vaccinated against it.

**Newcastle disease** This causes a nervous respiratory disorder. Symptoms include nasal discharge, excessive mucus in the trachea, and difficulty in breathing. Particularly in young birds, nervous disorders, such as paralysis of one or both wings and legs or a twisting of the neck and head, may also develop. Mortality rates vary and vaccines are available.

## PROTOZOAN DISEASES

**Coccidiosis** This is characterized by diarrhea, lethargy, and emaciation. It is usually seen in growing birds and young adults. Most poultry feeds contain a coccidiostat, which prevents any outbreak.

## EXTERNAL PARASITES

Mites and lice are the two most common external parasites of poultry. These pests can transmit pathogens, decrease egg production, affect appetite, reduce weight gain, and even lead to death. To help prevent infestation, keep the henhouse as clean as possible and discourage any contact with outside flocks of chickens. Wild birds and vermin can also spread these parasites and therefore you should prevent any close contact with your poultry or their housing. It is advisable to examine members of the flock from time to time for signs of infestation.

**Mites** These are usually found on and under feathers but a few varieties may be found in body tissues, feather quills, and respiratory passages. Some mites, such as the northern fowl mite, de-pluming mite, and chicken mite, live on the host and are usually detected by damaged feathers and feather loss. Other species, such as the red mite, hide around roosts during the day and feed on the host only at night, making them difficult to detect. The scaly-leg mite burrows beneath the scales on feet and legs, causing large, disfiguring crusts and scabs to form. You can remedy most infestations with viscous oil applications to afflicted birds' legs.

**Lice** These are wingless insects with flattened bodies and broadly rounded heads. There are several species of lice that affect chickens, including the body louse, the head louse, the wing louse, and the fluff louse. Checking under chickens' feathers regularly for signs of infestation is the best form of detection, as is watching out for egg clusters on downy feathers, especially on the head and around the vent.

## INTERNAL PARASITES

**Roundworms** Large roundworms are a common parasite of poultry. Adult worms are 1½ –3 inches (4–7.5 cm) long and the diameter of a pencil lead. Treatment is by prevention; clean the henhouses thoroughly before introducing any new birds.

**Tapeworms** These are flattened, ribbon-shaped worms composed of numerous segments. They vary in size from very small to several inches in length. All poultry tapeworms spend part of their lives in intermediate hosts (usually insects), and birds become infected by eating these hosts. Although several drugs are available for removing tapeworms, most are of doubtful efficacy.

**Cecal worms** This parasite is rarely problematic, though severe infestations may cause weakness and emaciation. Phenothiazine and hygromycin B are good as treatments.

## SOME HEALTHY ADVICE

**1** Don't run new chickens in facilities previously used by another flock until the facilities have been cleaned and disinfected.
**2** Never mix chicks or growing birds with adults.
**3** If strangers are introduced into a flock, quarantine them for several weeks to ensure they are disease free.
**4** Try to avoid undue exposure of a flock to wild birds or vermin.
**5** Feed a well-balanced diet as this will aid ability to resist disease.
**6** Try to make housing as roomy as possible with good ventilation.
**7** Isolate any sick birds.
**8** Vaccinate against disease.
**9** Guard against parasites but expect to find them during inspections.
**10** Work closely with your veterinarian.

# CHAPTER TWO

# Keeping Ducks

There are many reasons for keeping ducks. Not only are they a pleasure to look after and attractive to look at and produce abundant eggs for eating but they will also entertain you with their antics. Ducks are sometimes referred to as the gardener's friend as they eat slugs and snails. There are many breeds of duck and they come in a wide range of different shapes and sizes, several of which are suitable for keeping on a small scale.

# Who's who in ducks

## MUSCOVY

### Origin and characteristics

The Muscovy originated in Brazil and was domesticated in Europe about 1559. Technically, it is a member of the goose family, since it grazes and eats grass. It is also known as the Barbary duck. Unlike other ducks, it goes broody and will sit on and hatch eggs of other breeds. It flies and perches on roosts and trees. If already mated with its own breed, it will not mate with other breeds. Where cross-matings are successful, the crossbred progeny are infertile and are known as mules. Both males and females hiss rather than quack.

### Eggs

Muscovies are poor egg producers and lay their eggs in clutches – they may lay twenty or so eggs and go broody or pause before producing again.

**Above:** *Muscovy ducks*

### FACT FILE

**HEAD**
■ Compared with the rest of its body, the head is rather large. The face is feather-free. There are red caruncles on the face and at the top of the bill.

**BODY**
■ The body, slightly arched on top, tends to be rectangular. Muscovies walk rather slowly, with a horizontal carriage. In laying ducks, the abdomen tends to sag. The drake has no curl feathers in the tail.

**LEGS**
■ Shanks and feet are orange. The former are rather short and thick.

**COLOR**
■ White, black, black with white wings.

# AYLESBURY

## FACT FILE

**HEAD**
■ Large, straight and long. The white or flesh-colored bill is 6–8 inches (15–20 cm) long and almost straight in line with the top of the skull.

**BODY**
■ The breast should be very prominent and the body long, broad and deep. The tail is only slightly curved. The keel bone should be practically parallel with the ground and the carriage horizontal. This breed moves with a slow waddling gait.

**LEGS**
■ Well set to balance the body and short, strong and bright orange.

**COLOR**
■ The pure white plumage should be bright and glossy.

### Origin and characteristics

Fanciers often claim that there are very few purebred Aylesbury ducks left and that what is commonly termed an Aylesbury is, in fact, a Pekin. The Aylesbury is often crossed with the hardier Pekin to produce a stronger, more vigorous duck.

### Eggs

Although the Aylesburys are not good layers, they do lay better than Muscovies and do not go broody. Their eggs are a greenish-white.

**Above:** *Aylesbury ducks*

# PEKIN

### Origin and characteristics

This hardy breed of duck originated in China and is now the most numerous meat breed in North America, Great Britain and Australia.

### Eggs

Although mainly kept for commercial meat production, Pekins are better egg producers than the Muscovy and Aylesbury. Like the Aylesbury, Pekins seldom go broody. They are a nervous breed and need to be handled carefully so that their egg production and rate of weight gain are not affected.

**Above:** *Pekin ducks*

## FACT FILE

**HEAD**

■ Large, broad and round. The bright orange bill is short, broad, thick and slightly coarse. Eyes are partially shaded by heavy eyebrows and are dark lead blue. Neck is long and thick, and carried well forward in a graceful curve, with a slight gullet in the throat.

**BODY**

■ The stern should be carried just clear of the ground. The tail should be well spread and carried high; in the drake, it has two or three curled feathers on top. The chest is prominent and the carriage upright, sloping down at the rear.

**LEGS**

■ Strong and set well back to allow for the erect carriage of the body. The legs and feet are bright orange.

**COLOR**

■ The plumage is a uniform deep cream or buff canary color. Bright yellows generally indicate yellow flesh.

# INDIAN RUNNER

## FACT FILE

### HEAD
■ A wedge-shaped bill. Skull is flat on top. Alert eyes set high. The fine, long and graceful neck is carried almost in line with the body.

### BODY
■ Slim, cylindrical and long. Carriage is almost perpendicular to ground.

### LEGS
■ Thighs are longer and stronger than in other breeds. Legs must be set well back on the body to allow for upright carriage.

### COLOR
■ **Fawn:** body, legs and feet are yellowish brown.

■ **White:** plumage is pure white; bill, legs and feet are orange.

■ **Fawn and white:** a white line divides bill from head and runs from eyes to neck. Another white area extends from the breast, between the legs. The rest of the body is fawn. The bill, legs and feet are orange.

### Origin and characteristics
Another hardy breed, the Indian Runner originally came from the East Indies (Malaysia and China) and is an ancestor of the Khaki Campbell. The most popular and common varieties are the fawn, the white, and the fawn and white. The other two varieties are the black and the chocolate. Apart from its small frame, the breed is distinguished by its unusual almost upright stance and the running gait from which its name is derived.

### Eggs
The Indian Runner is a first-class egg producer.

### Management
Indian Runners do not require a pond, unlike many ducks, and will be content with a large tub for immersing their heads.

**Above:** *Indian Runner ducks*

# ROUEN

### Origin and characteristics

The Rouen, originally from France, is the least popular of table breeds because it is the slowest to mature and has dark flesh. Its most outstanding feature is its magnificent color and markings, a throwback to the Mallard from which it originated. The female differs in color from the male and lays quite well.

## FACT FILE

**HEAD**
■ The head is massive; the bill is long, wide, flat and bright greenish-yellow, with a black bean at the top. The neck is slightly curved.

**BODY**
■ The body is square, long and broad, with a very deep breast. The carriage is horizontal, with the keel parallel to and just clear of the ground.

**LEGS**
■ The brick-red legs are medium length and well set to balance the body.

**COLOR**
■ The drake's head and upper neck are rich iridescent green with a white ring that divides the neck and breast colors. The breast is a rich claret. A penciling effect is created by grey feathers on the underpart and sides; the back and tail are rich greenish-black. The duck's head and neck are rich brown; the rest of the plumage is a similar color, with either black or greenish-black penciling.

# KHAKI CAMPBELL

### Origin and characteristics

The Khaki Campbell was originally bred by Mrs. Adele Campbell in England, by crossing a Rouen drake with a fawn and white Indian Runner duck to establish a dual-purpose breed that has since spread all over the world.

### Eggs

The Khaki Campbell is quite hardy and it lays eggs with a pearly white shell. It is the best egg layer, producing over 300 eggs annually, and is therefore a popular choice for egg production.

## FACT FILE

**HEAD**
■ Carried high and rather fine in texture. Neck is slender and carried almost erect and the bill is set nearly in a straight line with the top of the skull.

**BODY**
■ Deep, compact, and fairly wide. The back is slightly sloping with the abdomen well developed but not sagging; carriage is slightly upright. Bird should be free from coarseness.

**COLOR**
■ The head and neck of the drake are greenish and the rest of its body is khaki brown. Bill is dark green, legs and feet are dark orange. Immature drakes are the same color as ducks. Duck's body is an even khaki color, as are legs and feet; bill is greenish-black.

# What do ducks need?

## HOUSING

There is no need to buy or make a really sophisticated duck house as, unlike chickens, ducks do not need windows, nest boxes, or perches. The most important considerations are good ventilation and a dry floor. Whatever housing you choose, whether it is a purpose-built duck house or a converted disused building, it should face north to northeast and be at least 6 feet (2 m) high at the back, to give enough head room. Since all ducks are very susceptible to excessive sun, adequate shade must be provided. Allow an area of at least 1 sq yd (1 sq m) per five birds of floor space.

The simplest form of duck house is a light apex-type wooden construction that can be moved around to provide fresh grazing. It should have wire mesh doors and be sited within a securely fenced run to protect the ducks from predators. It must be easily accessible for cleaning and the doors should always be secured at night.

## FENCING

It is usually necessary to fence the grazing area, pasture or fields to which ducks have access. Most woven wire field fencing is of small enough mesh to confine birds. Two-in (five-cm) mesh poultry netting is most commonly used for younger birds. The fence does not need to be particularly high since ducks seldom fly. An adequate height would be 3 ft (1 m). However, to protect your ducks from foxes, you might consider erecting a 6-ft (2-m) high heavy wire fence with a 12-in (30-cm) overlap at the top. Some people give their ducks the run of the yard as they don't scratch the earth or damage plants.

**Above:** *This attractive White Crested duck is protected from any would-be predators, such as dogs, by a high wire fence.*

## Flooring

The wooden floor should be covered with wood shavings or clean, dry straw to a depth of about 4 in (10 cm) for the comfort of the birds, to absorb moisture and to prevent egg breakage. Clean out the bedding and replace it with fresh twice a week, especially in wet weather. To keep the floor dry, raise it slightly off the ground and provide a running board for the ducks to enter by. This will also help to deter rats.

## Ventilation

The duck house should be well ventilated and you can achieve this by providing a wire mesh door or wire mesh sections at the top of the duck house.

## DUCKLINGS

Ducklings must have a permanent supply of good clean drinking water. You can provide refillable inverted glass jars for the first few days and then an automatic bell-type hanging waterer. Ducklings should be able to immerse their heads in the water but must not be allowed to swim in it. To avoid damp litter, you should place waterers on a wire grid over the concrete floor. Ducklings can die if they go without water for even relatively short periods. Staggering and convulsions are the typical symptoms of lack of water.

## Nests

Ducks do not need nest boxes but it is always a good idea to encourage your ducks to use nests because cleaner eggs are produced and fewer breakages occur. Furthermore, eggs laid in nests are not exposed to the sun or damp. This may be difficult with breeds other than Muscovy ducks, which go broody and will sit on and hatch eggs. Nests should always be clean, dry and comfortable and only large enough to be used by one duck at a time. Timber is a good material for building nest boxes and you should place them in rows along the walls of the duck house. A suitable size is about 12 in (30 cm) square and 18 in (45 cm) deep.

## Feeders

As a general rule, ducks need twice as much feeding space as hens. Trough feeders are the most satisfactory types for ducks. Provide each duck with a feeding space of at least 6 in (15 cm).

## Waterers

Although swimming water is not really necessary, ducks do need unlimited clean drinking water. Birds should be able to immerse their heads completely and thus clean and prevent blockage of their nasal passages with food and dirt.

Keep drinking containers shaded at all times. Again, to prevent damp litter, place drinking vessels outside the shed or on a wire grid. Provide about 2 in (5 cm) of drinking space for each adult bird.

## FEEDING YOUR DUCKS

Ducks can be fed on both mash and pelleted feed but crumbles and pellets are more economical because less feed is wasted and weight gains are better. Mash also tends to stick to ducks' bills, causing some birds to choke. Crumbles or pellets can be placed in hoppers so that the ducks have access to them at all times, or wet mash may be fed twice daily. Each duck will eat about 8 oz (225 g) of feed a day. Provide about forty percent of this in the morning feed and sixty percent in the evening feed. Ducks must have access to unlimited soluble grit.

**Below:** *These Pekin ducks have a large bowl of fresh water in which they can immerse their heads completely.*

## DIGGING A POND

A pond is not absolutely essential. All that most ducks need is a large tub in which to immerse their heads completely. However, ducks seem to be happier when they have a pond, and swimming water also aids feathering.

Good drainage is essential. Since most ducks lay their eggs in the evening and early mornings, it is advisable to prevent outside swimming until about 10.00 A.M., when most eggs will have been laid.

There are several things to consider, however, before starting to dig a pond if you do not already have one. The first consideration is how it will be cleaned. If it is a large farm pond, it should be periodically flushed, especially if stocking twenty to thirty birds. This can be done

with well water or naturally flowing water. The maximum number of ducks is 100 per acre of water. Excessive numbers

**Below:** *These handsome Muscovy ducks live beside a pond. To protect them from predators, they are shut in the duck house at night.*

of ducks rapidly pollute the water and the edges of the pond are quickly destroyed by their dabbling habit.

Smaller ponds are best if they are cement lined with a drain in the bottom, or you can even use a fiberglass mold. It is also wise to have an overflow pipe so if

**Above:** *Like most ducks, Indian Runners will enjoy swimming if you have a pond or stream.*

the pond becomes too full, the excess water is skimmed off by the overflow pipe and does not spill over the edges. Gravel or sand should be spread around the pond borders so less mud and mess are produced. However, you must ensure that the gravel is not too sharp or it could damage the ducks' feet.

The banks of the pond should not be too steep so provide a gentle slope to allow the ducks easy access.

## POND PLANTS

Ducks will eat almost any plant, especially if it is the only vegetation around. The following plants seem to be the most hardy if planted in a waterfowl pen.

**In their pen, plant the following:**
- Ground ivy (*Glechoma hederacea*)
- Silverweed (*Potentilla anserina*)
- Camomile species (*Matricaria*)
- Large-leafed butterbur (*Petasites*)

**On the pond edge, try planting:**
- Day lilies (*Hemercallis*)
- Yellow iris (*Iris pseudacorus*)
- Tall perennial grass euialia (*miscanthus*)

**For nests:**
- Stinging nettle (*Urtica dioica*)
- Butterbur (*Petasites*)
- Smartweed

**For protection from wind and sun:**
- Low-growing conifers
- Chinese Juniper
- Dwarf Pine

# What do I do?

## EGG PRODUCTION AND HANDLING

The egg production of ducks can vary tremendously due to their genetics and management. The management factors that most affect egg production are:

■ Good quality of feed.

■ Proper quantity of feed — for maximum production ducks must have limited feed from three weeks of age until they are laying well — no more than 5 oz (142 g) of feed per duck per day for the larger strains. Once they are laying well they can have as much as they want to eat.

■ Proper lighting — an increasing day length (January to June in the northern hemisphere) brings sexually mature ducks into egg production, and a decreasing day length (July to December in the northern hemisphere) slows or stops their egg production. To prevent this happening, you can supplement the natural light with artificial light in the morning and evening so the laying duck has seventeen total hours of light a day.

### Egg collection

Most ducks lay their eggs during the night or early morning. Eggs must be gathered first thing to prevent them becoming dirty and to keep any breakages to a minimum. Ducks engaged in laying during collection should be left on the nest. Dirty eggs should be kept separate from clean eggs during collection to avoid any cross-contamination. They must be cleaned immediately after collection to prevent penetration of the shell by harmful microbes. Lightly rub them with fine-grade steel wool to remove dry mud and manure. The eggs may then be wiped with a clean damp cloth.

### Storage

Eggs will probably need to be stored until there are enough to incubate. The longer the eggs are kept, the less chance they have of hatching; the likelihood of hatching decreases after seven days. It is most unlikely that ducklings will be hatched from eggs kept for three weeks, even under the best storage conditions.

Egg storage temperatures are critical. Ideally, they should be stored at 55°F (13°C) with a relative humidity of seventy-five percent. Low temperatures can cause the embryo to die, whereas high temperatures can start incubation. Store eggs with the pointed end down. If they are to be kept longer than seven days, turn them daily through an angle of ninety degrees.

## NATURAL INCUBATION

Although some ducks will sit on their eggs and make good mothers, many breeds are not very reliable. Muscovy

ducks can be used to incubate and hatch out their own or any other breed of duck and can easily cover up to sixteen eggs. Ducks sitting on eggs should exercise daily and be provided with food and water near their nest. Both English breeds and the Muscovies can be satisfactorily hatched out under broody hens.

### Rearing baby ducklings

Rearing the baby ducklings is not difficult. For smaller numbers all that is needed is a large cardboard box, some shavings or straw, a heat lamp, a feeder and a waterer. As they grow, they will need more space and less heat. Observe the birds — if they stay away from the heat, turn it off — if they get their pen messy rapidly, they need more bedding and more space. By five or six weeks they can probably be outside all the time in fine weather but it is a good idea to

**Above:** *Since Aylesbury ducks are usually bred for meat, they tend to be moderate layers.*

partially cover the run when the ducklings are young to help keep them dry and provide shade on sunny days.

## ARTIFICIAL INCUBATION

All breeds hatch in twenty-eight days with the exception of the Muscovy, which takes thirty-five days. The incubator room need not be elaborate but it must be adequately ventilated and able to maintain a constant temperature under all conditions. Run the incubator for a full day before setting, to test if it is working properly and to build up and maintain the desired temperature. Remove the eggs from cool storage to room temperature six hours before setting as this will prevent a sudden rise in temperature when placed in the incubator.

Transfer the eggs, with the pointed end down, to incubator trays. Set the incubator to run at 99°F (37.5°C) and maintain this temperature throughout incubation but reduce it by 32°F (0.2°C) in the hatchers.

## BROODING

Ducklings can be brooded in any reasonable brooder accommodation and under any type of brooder used for chickens. Brooders should provide enough constant heat and space beneath it to avoid overcrowding. As a general rule, the number of ducklings that can be brooded is half the stated chick capacity of a brooder. Where hanging brooders are used, surrounds should be placed on the floor space immediately below the source of warmth and gradually moved a little further away from the brooder each day, until removal by the end of the first week.

For the first week, the temperature of the brooder should be 86°F (30°C), gradually reducing by 5°F each week until the third week, when the heat may be switched off (depending on the weather). Ducklings may have access to outside runs from about ten days of age, but they cannot tolerate rain until they are about three to four weeks old, when they have enough feathers. They must also be protected from predators, such as rats, foxes, and dogs.

Too much humidity prevents eggs from drying out sufficiently while too little causes the contents to dry out too quickly. You can control the humidity by adjusting the ventilators of the machine and by using moisture trays. High humidity will give the best results.

### Turning the eggs

Always turn the eggs through an angle of ninety degrees. This will allow free movement of the embryo and prevent the contents from sticking to the shell.

### Candling

Eggs are candled by shining an electric light through them so their contents can be seen and embryonic development determined. Eggs may be tested for fertility on day seven. Infertile eggs are clear, and a dead embryo shows as a dark spot stuck to the shell membrane. Remove any infertile eggs and eggs containing dead embryos from the trays.

### Taking off the hatch

As soon as possible after the hatch is completed, transfer the ducklings to the brooders. Some causes of poor hatches include incorrect operation of the incubator, faulty management of the breeding flock, poor nutrition, and genetic weaknesses in the breeding stock. Ducks can vary in hatchability between sixty and seventy-five percent, depending upon the age of the flock and general management conditions.

# What to expect

## MATING

First-year ducks and drakes perform best but must not be less than six months of age. The number of ducks to one drake is governed by the breed, age, and the method of management. With the heavy breeds, such as the Muscovy, a ratio of one drake to five ducks is required. With the lighter breeds, such as the Khaki Campbell, one drake to ten ducks may do.

The number of birds to be mated depends on the number of ducklings you require. With most breeds, one duck can produce about 100 ducklings per season. To give both ducks and drakes time to settle down, they should be mated for two weeks before eggs are collected for setting. This will enable proper mating to occur and help ensure high fertility in eggs laid.

## PARASITES

The most common internal parasite is the large roundworm (*Ascaridia galli*), which should be controlled by the periodic administration of a recommended treatment to either the ducks' feed or water. Ask your veterinarian for advice.

## DISEASES

Ducks are fairly disease resistant when good husbandry and management techniques are followed. By taking positive measures to prevent disease (housing, feeding, and rearing your ducks properly) and buying in new stock from a good breeder with healthy stock, you can be reasonably confident that your ducks should have a high resistance to disease. However, leg weakness, cholera, botulism, mycosis, non-specific diarrhea, salmonellosis, sinusitis, spirochetosis, rickets, vitamin A deficiency, and white eye sometimes occur. If you suspect any of these, consult your veterinarian. If one of your ducks does become sick or off-color, you should isolate it immediately as a precautionary measure.

**Left:** *When breeding Crested ducks you can see the quality of the crest immediately when the ducklings hatch out.*

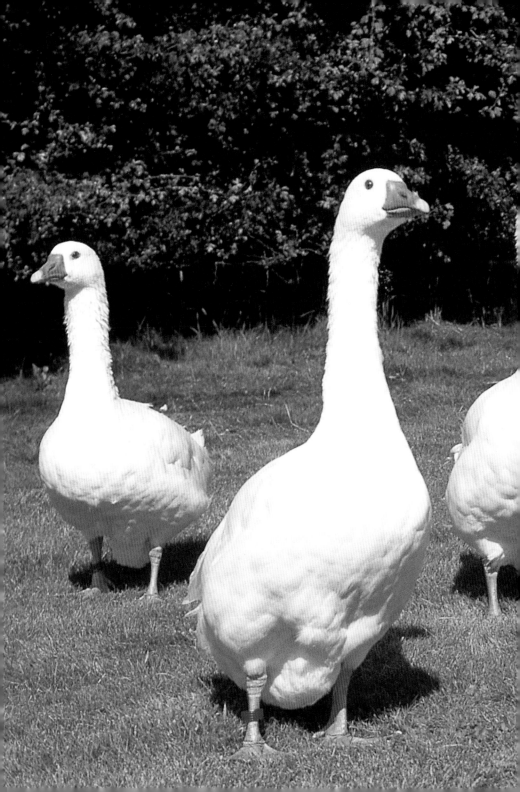

# CHAPTER THREE

# Keeping Geese

There are lots of good reasons for keeping geese. Not only can they perform useful guard duties, crop the grass, and produce large eggs but they are also attractive to look at and can be extremely entertaining animals. Although geese are not prolific egg producers, they are the most rapidly growing of all waterfowl, have the longest life and are the hardiest of all domesticated birds.

# History and origins

Historically geese were often kept as a convenient source of sacrificial offerings to the gods. Their feathers were used for writing purposes and their down for pillows and covers. At certain times of year, geese were literally walked in large flocks by their producers to the nearby marketplace and therefore lighter breeds were preferred. The decline in their number and popularity is widespread to the point where large flocks of geese are now a relatively uncommon sight.

This decline can be attributed in part to the rise of the ballpoint pen, man-made fiber fillings for soft-furnishings, and a shift in eating habits toward leaner, whiter meats. However, geese remain popular as pets and as adornments to farmyard ponds as well as in backyard systems where they are most frequently seen living in pairs or foursomes.

**Below:** *Hawaiian geese, with their distinctive striped markings, are gaining in popularity despite the fact that they were on the verge of extinction fifty years ago.*

# Who's who in geese

## EMBDEN

### FACT FILE

**HEAD**
■ Long and straight.
The bill is short and
stout at the base, the
eyes bold and light
blue and the neck is
long and swan-like.

**BODY**
■ The Embden's body
is broad, thick and well
rounded. The breast is
round and the back
long and straight. The
legs are fairly short but
strong and the carriage
upright.

**COLOR**
■ The bill, legs and
feet are bright orange,
and the hard, tight
plumage is pure glossy
white.

### Origin and characteristics

The Embden is a heavy, hardy breed that originates from
Hanover in Germany. It is a prolific breeder and has a
quiet disposition. Because their feathers are white, they
are of greater value than feathers from other geese.
Goslings can be sexed at a day old with a reasonable
degree of accuracy, as females have a darker down than
males. Although these geese do not require housing,
they must be protected from predators, especially foxes,
so you will need to build an enclosure with predator-
proof fencing to protect them at night.

### Eggs

The Embden produces up to forty eggs per season, sits
well, matures early and is a good forager.

**Above:** *Embden geese*

# CHINESE

### Origin and characteristics

There are brown and white varieties of this light breed. It originated in China and is smaller than the Toulouse or the Embden. The hardy Chinese is distinguishable from other geese by the knob or protuberance on its head. It is also the most suitable "watchdog" breed.

### Eggs

Chinese geese go broody and are good layers, laying as many as fifty eggs in a season and because of this they have proved ideal for crossing with other breeds.

**Above:** *Chinese geese*

## FACT FILE

### HEAD
■ This is rather large with a knob at the base of the upper bill.

### BODY
■ No particular distinguishing features except that it is smaller than the Toulouse and Embden.

### COLOR
■ **Brown variety:** Brown bill and eyes, orange legs. The body feathers are brown and they are lighter on the underside of the bird.
■ **White variety:** Bright orange bill and legs, brown eyes, and pure white body feathers.

# TOULOUSE

## FACT FILE

**WEIGHT**
■ Gander: 26 lb (12 kg)

■ Goose: 20 lb (9 kg)

**HEAD**
■ This is strong and massive. The bill is strong and short, the eyes brown and the neck long and thick with plenty of gullet in the throat.

**BODY**
■ The Toulouse's body is long, broad, and deep with a very prominent breast bone. The back curves slightly from neck to tail and the carriage is horizontal. The Toulouse needs plenty of space for exercising to prevent it becoming fat.

**COLOR**
■ The bill, legs and feet are orange. The plumage varies through different shades of gray with each feather laced with a white edging. The stern, paunch, and tail are white.

### Origin and characteristics

The Toulouse is one of the heavy breeds originating from France where it is kept primarily for its fat liver and for pâté production. For mating purposes, the Toulouse must have access to water, preferably a natural pond or stream.

### Eggs

Some strains are non-broody and, of the heavy breeds, the Toulouse is only an average layer, producing up to thirty-five eggs per season.

**Above:** *Toulouse goose*

# OTHER BREEDS

## ROMAN

The Roman originated in Europe from the Toulouse and Embden, resembling the Embden more strongly. It is thought to be the oldest of the European breeds. With its pure white plumage, it is a handsome-looking goose although it is inclined to be noisier than many other breeds.

**Below:** *Roman geese*

## AFRICAN

The African breed is a variety of the Chinese; it is slightly larger because of an infusion of Toulouse, giving the breed a dewlap. The breed possibly originated in India but is not as good an egg producer as the Chinese goose.

## SEBASTOPOL

The Sebastopol is basically a fancy breed and it has increased in both number and popularity in the last few years with backyard keepers. It has long, curved white feathers on its back with short, white curled feathers on the lower part of the body.

## GREY BACK

This medium-sized goose has a gray head with the color extending down its neck and a gray mantle on the back.

**Above:** *Grey Back goose*

## DIEPHOLZ

This attractive white goose comes from Northern Germany, from the region of Diepholz. It has been bred there for the past 100 years. In 1925 the Diepholz was recognised as a breed and is in build and appearance very close to the Grey goose.

## PILGRIM

This calm, personable goose is the only breed where the male and female come in different colors; the males are creamy white and the females are olive-gray. It is often described as an old breed, having originated in England and arrived in North America with the Pilgrim Fathers, but it is likely that the goose was not standardized as a breed until the 1930s. Whatever the truth of its origins, the Pilgrim makes a superior home goose because of its quiet disposition, excellent parenting qualities, and fast growth.

## ROSS' GOOSE

Ross' geese are the smallest goose species with white plumage and a relatively short neck. They have a rapid wing beat.

**Below:** *Ross' geese*

# What do they need?

Geese obtain approximately eighty percent of their food from grass so they do need plenty of room for grazing. Space is a prime consideration if you plan to keep some geese as five adult geese will need at least one-quarter of an acre of good-quality pasture.

## HOUSING

Sheds for housing geese need only a simple pent roof but it is essential that the accommodation can be completely enclosed and always locked at night for protection against foxes and other predators. Always shut your geese up before dusk and don't let them out until the following morning.

You can buy a purpose-built wooden goose house or can adapt some existing outbuildings, such as stables. Use wire mesh doors and windows for ventilation.

A 4-in (10-cm) layer of wood shavings on the floor will help maintain dry conditions. A concrete floor may be needed, depending on the climate and drainage. Geese tend to foul their sleeping quarters, so you must remove damp and wet litter frequently.

## PASTURE (FREE-RANGE)

If geese are to be kept extensively on pasture, then it is not essential to provide birds with houses. However, they will need a fenced fox-proof enclosure, some shade for hot weather, and shelter, such as straw bales or hurdles.

## FEEDING ADULT GEESE

Geese should have access to both soluble and insoluble grit at all times. Soluble grit is in the form of limestone chips (5 mm) or shell grit, while insoluble grit is usually

**Left:** *A purpose-built goose house will keep your birds safe at night.*

supplied as blue metal or basalt chips screened to 5–6 mm. You could also try layers' pellets, barley, or wheat.

## FEEDING BREEDING GEESE

Good grazing for all breeding stock will be needed for up to six weeks before the breeding season. Up to and during the breeding season, feed geese a ration with about 16 percent protein. Rations for laying hens are suitable. Breeding geese in full lay should be given about 7 oz (200 g) of prepared feed a day, depending on the amount of pasture or green feed available.

## FEEDING GOSLINGS

Goslings are often fed a similar ration to ducks, but because goslings show a rapid weight gain during the first four weeks, they need more protein. The heavy breeds of geese weigh approximately 3–3½ oz (85–100 g) at a day old and may weigh up to 3½ lb (1.6 kg) at four weeks. Provided there is plenty of green feed, they can begin to graze at a few weeks.

The live weight of geese will increase by up to fifty percent during their first two months of life. Goslings grow more rapidly when they are housed and fed a completely prepared and well-balanced ration than when they graze. Goslings reared in cages will weigh up to twenty percent more than floor-reared goslings, to ten weeks of age. Day-old birth weight and rate of growth in the first month

influence a gosling's weight at ten weeks.

A starter diet containing twenty percent protein is recommended for the first month in conjunction with good grazing.

## PASTURE AND GRAZING

Geese are more like grazing animals than any other type of poultry. Because they have virtually no crop in which to hold their feed, they tend to feed and graze frequently. In summer they may continue to graze and feed at night. Their beak and tongue are particularly well-equipped for grazing. The beak has sharp interlocking serrated edges designed to cut and divide grass and other plant tissue easily. The tongue at the tip is covered with hard, hair-like projections, pointing toward the throat, which quickly convey the pieces of grass and other vegetable material into the throat. This rough covering on the point of the tongue enables geese to bite off plants even closer to the ground than sheep can. Because of this, you must avoid overstocking or the ground will become bare. The stocking density for geese on pasture will vary depending on the quality of the pasture and the age and size of the geese.

Goslings can start grazing at just a few weeks of age. If your pasture is good and plentiful then you should reduce the amount of prepared food you give them. Try practicing a system of rotational grazing to ensure that your geese have access to good pasture all the time. Where paddocks are fenced off, the pasture will recover quickly and the grazing will be more hygienic.

If pasture for grazing is not available, then you should feed the breeders chopped green feed. Geese prefer to pick their own green feed and may reject cut grass unless it is fresh and very finely chopped.

Geese can be very selective in the pasture they eat and tend to pick out the more palatable pastures. They reject narrow-leaved tough grasses and select the more succulent clover and grasses. During the nonbreeding season, breeding geese only need access to pasture to satisfy their total feed requirements.

**Below:** *These noble-looking Roman geese are allowed to roam free-range and are grazing under a clump of shady trees.*

# What do I do?

## HATCHING

Natural incubation will produce the best percentage of goslings hatched. Since geese are not laying while they are sitting on the eggs, hens and Muscovy ducks may be used to hatch out the goslings.

Eggs should be collected at least twice (preferably four times) daily and, as geese lay most of their eggs in the morning, the bulk of them should be collected then.

Eggs for incubation should be stored in a cool room at 59°F (15°C); it may be worth investing in an air-conditioned or refrigerated cabinet as this is ideal. You must turn the eggs daily. The longer that they are kept over seven days, the poorer the hatching results. You should select only the uncracked eggs that weigh at least 5 oz (140 g) and no more than 7 oz (200 g). Clean the eggs by lightly rubbing them with some steel wool and then wiping with a clean damp cloth. You need to wash them thoroughly in warm water with a disinfectant, or fumigate them immediately after collection.

The actual period of incubation of goose eggs varies slightly with the breed. Some eggs from the lighter breeds may start hatching after twenty-eight days, while eggs from the larger breeds, such as the Toulouse and Embden, may take thirty-five days. It may take up to three days for hatching to be completed.

## INCUBATION

**Natural**
Depending on the size of the bird, four to six eggs may be placed under a broody hen while a Muscovy duck may sit on six to eight eggs. Since the eggs are too large for most hens to turn, turning the eggs by hand is necessary on a daily basis when the hens leave the nest to eat and drink. After fifteen days, sprinkle the eggs with lukewarm water every time you turn them. Candling – passing the eggs under a bright electric light to view their contents – can be done on the tenth day; all infertile eggs must be removed.

Where a goose is to be used for hatching out the eggs, you can place ten to fifteen eggs – depending on their size and the size of the goose – underneath her. If your geese have access to some swimming facilities, the eggs need not be sprinkled with water.

**Artificial**
Artificial incubation can be used but, unless machines are properly managed, goose eggs do not hatch very well; often no more than forty percent of the eggs set. With forced draft machines, a constant temperature of 99°F (37.5°C) throughout the incubation period is required. The desired humidity will be obtained if the wet bulb thermometer is

## Handling geese

Always catch geese by the neck, never by the legs, which are weak and easily injured or broken. To hold or carry a goose, first catch it by the neck, either with a hand or a catching hook. Then pull the bird close to your body. Reach down with the other arm and wrap it around the bird's body, holding the wings in place and grasping both legs with one finger between the legs. Lift the bird onto your arm and move the goose to the side of your body, so the head and neck protrude from under your arm.

kept at a reading of 90°F (32.2°C) to the twenty-ninth day. Increase it to 93°F (34°C) for the rest of the incubation, adjusting the ventilation.

The best results are obtained if the eggs are set horizontally and turned at least four times daily, through an angle of 180 degrees.

Goose eggs require high humidity, so sprinkle them daily with warm water. After the fifteenth day, submerge them every second day in water kept at a temperature of 99°F (37.5°C) and then daily in the last week of incubation for one minute.

Transfer them to the hatcher on the twenty-seventh day. They should be dipped or sprinkled with water only once after they are transferred. The temperature should be kept at 98°F (37°C) and relative humidity at about eighty percent. After the peak of the hatch, reduce to 97°F (36.5°C) and seventy percent humidity. Leave goslings in the hatcher for two to four hours after the hatch is completed, and then transfer to the brooders.

## Brooding and rearing

If only small numbers of goslings are to be raised, you can use a Muscovy duck or broody hen to hatch them. Leave them in the care of the bird that hatched them out to avoid using artificial heat. A hen can care for up to six goslings. The hen or duck should be confined to a coop within a well-grassed yard for ten days.

They can also be reared satisfactorily under all types of brooders. Initially they need less heat than chickens and can fend for themselves earlier. In the first week, set the temperature of the brooder at about 86°F (30°C), then reduce it by 37–39°F (3–4°C) per week over the next two to three weeks. Keep the brooder accommodation clean and dry.

As goslings cannot tolerate wet conditions until they are partly feathered, do not give them access to swimming facilities until they are at least two weeks old. Move the coop daily to fresh ground and encourage the goslings to graze from three days onward. They will need plenty of shade and an adequate supply of good, clean drinking water at all times.

# What to expect

## BREEDING

Geese must be at least a year old before mating. They can be kept for breeding until they are ten years old but ganders are past their peak by the time they reach six years of age.

The number of geese to one gander varies; generally the more geese per gander the better, provided fertility and hatchability are not affected. Geese should be mated at least one month before the breeding season starts. With the heavier breeds, use one gander to three geese, and one to about five with the lighter Chinese breed.

Geese are selective in choosing their mates and, once successful matings have been established, will remain together for life. If the birds are allowed to select their own mates, it is best to put more than the required number in a pen until the selections have been made. To avoid fretting in the event of having to change mates, run the separated birds as far from each other as possible. There will be less fighting if ganders selected for breeding have been reared together.

Where flock matings are practiced, ganders may fight but no serious damage will occur if they are evenly matched. Bullies and birds that are continually subjected to bullying should be removed from the flock. So, too, should any geese that wander around on their own, as their eggs will be infertile.

## DISEASES

Like most waterfowl, geese are hardy birds and are not subject to many diseases. If a goose falls ill, you should consult your veterinarian, but this is unlikely if you buy healthy stock, feed them properly and keep their housing clean.

## EGG PRODUCTION

The main egg laying period for geese is in spring, although Chinese breeds can start laying in winter. Fertility will be up to fifteen percent higher and hatchability up to twenty percent higher with mature female geese than with one-year-old geese. As geese usually lay their eggs in the morning, make a late morning collection to reduce egg breakage. It's also best not to give geese access to swimming facilities until later in the morning, otherwise eggs may be lost. Geese usually lay a clutch of twelve to fifteen eggs and then go broody.

To reduce egg breakage, provide nest boxes and encourage their use for laying. Line them with suitable nesting material, such as shavings or straw, and allow one 20 x 20 in (50 x 50 cm) nest box for every three geese in the flock.

# CHAPTER FOUR

# Keeping Goats

The domesticated goat has played a central part in our lives for many thousands of years, providing milk, meat, and wool, particularly in arid, semi-tropical, or mountainous regions. In the more temperate zones, goats are more often kept as supplementary animals by smallholders, losing out in the dairy sector to cows or buffaloes and lagging behind sheep in the fiber and meat markets.

# Origins and evolution

Goats and sheep make up a tribe within the Bovidae family called Caprini, which includes six goat species distinguished by their horn shapes:

- The wild goat of Near East Asia
- The ibex of the Alps, Siberia, and Nubia
- The markhor of Central Asia
- The Spanish goat
- The Dagestan tur of the Caucasus
- The domestic goat, Angora, Cashmere, and Damascus goats.

Goats are thought to have evolved about twenty million years ago in the Miocene Age, much later than horses, donkeys, zebras, tapirs, and rhinoceroses, which make up the order of uneven-toed hoofed animals. All are herbivores who nurse their young from an external milk producing gland.

## MILK AND CHEESE PRODUCTION

Goat's milk and cheese production is now big business throughout the world with France, Greece, Norway, and Italy being renowned for their products. Sizeable goat herds are often an expression of wealth in Africa and Asia where goats are found in large numbers, and in the United States there are estimated to be between two and four million animals with Texas preeminent for Angora and bush goats, and California leading the way in dairy production.

Swiss breeds are the stars of milk production; Indian and Nubian-derived goats are dual-purpose meat and milk producers. The casein and fat content in goat's milk is more easily digested than cow's milk and is gentler on the stomachs of the elderly, sick, babies and young children. It is also preferable for raising orphan foals or puppies. Goat's milk fat globules are smaller and remain dispersed for longer than cow's milk and the milk is higher in vitamin A, niacin, choline, and inositol but lower in vitamins $B_6$, $B_{12}$, C, and carotenoids.

**Left:** *Goats are very sociable animals. They love company and like to see what's going on.*

# GOAT BREEDS

These vary greatly but the terminology remains the same for all breeds:
- Males are bucks
- Females are does
- Young goats are either buck or doe kids or doelings.

Some goats have horns of the scimitar or corkscrew type but many are artificially removed and some are naturally hornless. They can be short-haired, long-haired, curly-haired and silky, or coarse-wooled. They may have wattles on the neck and beards. Some breeds, particularly the Europeans, have straight noses whereas others have convex noses, like the Jamnapari and Nubian or the slightly dished nose of the Swiss. Whereas some breeds have erect ears, others have large, drooping ears; the American LaMancha breed has no external ear at all.

The main breeds of dairy goat are the Boer, Toggenburg, Saanen, Anglo-Nubian, Alpine, and the recent LaMancha, which was developed in California from Spanish Murciana origin and Swiss and Nubian crosses. It is renowned for its excellent adaptability and good winter production.

Angora goats originate from the Near East. The long upper coat (mohair) is a valuable product in contrast to cashmere, where the fine underwool is the prized asset. Pygmy goats are dwarf, short-legged goats from Western and Central Africa and the Caribbean. They are gaining

**Above:** *This young British Toggenburg male goat has its horns intact. If dehorned, they should be removed in the first seven days.*

wider acceptance on other continents but their growth rates and milk production are quite low. Most are kept as pets.

### Feral goats

Escaped or feral goats thrive nearly everywhere and are considered pests if they are uncontrolled. Truly wild goats are less common and are confined to places such as the Greek islands, Turkey, Iran, Pakistan, the Alps, Siberia, Sudan, the Pyrenees, the Himalayas, Central Asia, and the Russian and Tibetan mountain ranges as they prefer rocky mountains and cliffs. Goats cannot be herded by dogs as easily as sheep, tending to disperse and meet any threat head-on.

# Who's who in the goatherd?

## ALPINE

### Origin and characteristics

The French-Alpine is a breed of goat that originated in the Alps. Size and production rather than color pattern have been stressed in its development. The French-Alpine is also referred to as the Alpine Dairy goat. These are hardy, adaptable animals that thrive in any climate while maintaining good health and excellent milk production. Both sexes are generally short-haired but bucks usually have a roach of long hair along the spine. The beard of males is also quite pronounced. The ears of the Alpine should be of medium size, fine textured, and preferably erect. The face is straight with a Roman nose.

### Milk production

French-Alpine females are excellent milkers and usually have large, well-shaped udders with well-placed teats of desirable shape.

**Above:** *British Alpine*

### FACT FILE

**SIZE AND WEIGHT**

■ The French-Alpine is a larger and more rangy goat and more variable in size than the Swiss breeds.

■ The British Alpine is black with white markings.

■ Mature females should stand not less than 30 in (75 cm) at the withers and should weigh not less than 135 lb (61 kg).

■ Males should stand from 34–40 in (85–100 cm) at the withers and should weigh not less than 170 lb (77 kg).

**COLORS**

■ No standard color. Ranges between pure white, fawn, gray, brown, red, black, bluff, piebald. British Alpine is black and white.

# ANGLO-NUBIAN

## FACT FILE

### SIZE AND WEIGHT
■ A mature doe should stand at least 30 in (75 cm) at the withers and weigh 135 lb (61 kg) or more.

■ A male should stand at least 35 in (87.5 cm) at the withers and weigh at least 175 lb (80 kg).

### HEAD
■ A Roman nose and long pendulous ears hanging close to the head and flaring out and forward at the tip.

### COAT TYPE
■ Hair is short, fine and glossy – shorter on males.

### COLORS
■ Any color or combination of colors, solid or patterned, is acceptable within the definition of the breed.

### Origin and characteristics
The Anglo-Nubian derives its name from Nubia, in northeastern Africa. The original goats imported from Africa, Arabia and India were long-legged and hardy. English breeders crossed these imported bucks with common short-haired English does and the result is the Anglo-Nubian, sometimes referred to as the Nubian.

As it is the best suited of the dairy goat breeds to hot conditions, the bloodline has often been introduced into tropical countries to increase local milk production. The Anglo-Nubian is a relatively large, proud-looking and graceful dairy goat with a pendulous udder.

### Milk production
This all-purpose goat is not a heavy milker but its milk has a higher than average butter fat content (between four and five percent). The length of breeding season is longer than that of the Swiss breeds and so it is possible to produce year-round milk.

**Above:** *Anglo-Nubians*

# SAANEN

### Origin and characteristics

The majestic-looking Saanen dairy goat originated in Switzerland, in the Saanen Valley, and is one of the largest of the Swiss breeds. Sturdy and easy to keep, the Saanen has the capacity to tolerate environmental change, although the breed is sensitive to excessive sunlight and performs best in cooler conditions. The provision of shade is essential for these goats, especially during hot summers when they will seek shelter from the sun. They have a good resistance to disease, and the does should be feminine in feature and not coarse.

### Milk production

The Saanen and British Saanen does are heavy milk producers and usually yield three to four percent butter fat. They have good udder shapes.

**Above:** *British Saanen*

## FACT FILE

### SIZE AND WEIGHT
▓ Medium to large, weighing approx. 145 lb (66 kg), with rugged bone and plenty of vigor. They should stand at least 35 in (87 cm) at the withers.

### COAT TYPE
▓ Hair should be short and fine, although a fringe over the spine and thighs is often present.

### HEAD
▓ Ears should be erect and alertly carried, preferably pointing forward. The face should be straight or dished. Both the doe and buck have beards.

### COLORS AND MARKINGS
▓ White or light cream (white preferred). Spots on the skin are not discriminated against. Small spots of color on hair are allowable but not desirable.

# TOGGENBURG

### Origin and characteristics

The stylish Toggenburg is a Swiss dairy goat that hails from the Toggenburg Valley of Switzerland at Obertoggenburg. It is also credited as being the oldest known dairy goat breed. With its light fawn to dark chocolate coat and distinctive white markings, it is a handsome-looking goat. Cream, instead of white, markings are acceptable but not desirable. The nose and facial lines are concave, dished, or straight, but never Roman. The British Toggenburg is brown with white markings and is popular with goatkeepers.

### Milk production

The Toggenburg and British Toggenburg are both good, economical milkers, giving up to 6 pints (3.5 liters) daily. It has a capacious, soft, and pliable udder with well-formed and well-delineated teats.

**Above:** *British Toggenburg*

# ANGORA

### Origin and characteristics

The Angora originated in Asia Minor and is best known for mohair production. When mohair became fashionable in the nineteenth century, the Turks crossed the Angora with common stock to increase yields. Angoras were gradually imported into Western countries but none of these efforts was successful in establishing mohair production.

### Appearance

Both sexes are horned; the horns of mature bucks can reach 2 feet (60 cm). It is quite a delicate breed and susceptible to parasites.

## FACT FILE

**SIZE AND WEIGHT**
■ Small compared to dairy goats; considerable variation in their size.

■ Mature bucks weigh: 180–225 lb (82–102 kg).

■ Mature does weigh between: 70–110 lb (32–50 kg).

**COAT TYPE**
■ Classified according to type of ringlet in which hair grows. Ringlet-type goats are often referred to as C Types (the mohair is carried in tight ringlets and is the finest produced); B Types have a flat mohair coat. The flat lock is usually wavy and more bulky.

# PYGMY GOAT

**Above:** *Pygmy goats*

### Origin and characteristics

The Pygmy Goat was originally called the Cameroon Dwarf Goat. It was exported from Africa to zoos in Sweden and Germany and from there it made its way to England, Canada, and the United States. The offspring of these animals, as well as earlier imports, now make up the breed. They are mainly kept for the sheer fun of ownership.

## FACT FILE

**COAT TYPE**
■ A full coat of medium-long hair. Females seldom have beards. Males should have long, flowing beards.

**COLORS**
■ All body colors are acceptable. Grizzled agouti pattern predominates.

# What do they need?

If you are new to goatkeeping, you need to know the basic requirements that you must provide for your goats. These include adequate grazing, fencing, food, and housing. Misconceptions persist about goats and it is important to lay these to rest. Goats are a responsibility and demand commitment from you – they can't be left to roam freely and they will take up some of your free time as they will need feeding, fresh water, regular cleaning out, and daily milking.

**Below:** *Goats should range freely with access to good grazing and shrubby undergrowth.*

## GRAZING AND BROWSING

Goats browse for their food and are different from the other domesticated ruminants that are grazers. Under natural conditions, they are not great despoilers of vegetation because they will range over a wide area, selectively grazing and browsing. It is a myth that goats will eat anything; they are actually very particular about what they eat and will not consume poor-quality or dirty food. However, in confined conditions, goats will become heavy browsers of trees and shrubs, and be less discriminating in their

grazing habits because of the reduced supply.

They exhibit a definite preference for a varied diet, often consuming no less than twenty-five different plant species. This penchant serves the goat well because many so-called weeds have a higher mineral and protein content than grasses, owing to the greater root depth. This grazing behavior can also work as a bonus for you, the goatkeeper, as goats can be let out on land that has already been grazed by cattle and other livestock. In general, they prefer more fibrous food to lush grass, preferring to nibble young thistles and brambles, twigs, and the bark from trees. Thus, it is always a good idea to protect any trees that you value.

This may also help to explain why goats are less prone to bloat than most ruminants. They will never knowingly overgraze no matter how succulent the legumes. They will obtain the necessary roughage for normal rumen activity through browsing on pasture grasses and scrubby bushes.

### Grazing intake
This is related to the metabolic rate and body size of the goat, varying with the breed and age of the animal. The species and stage of growth of the plants being

**Below:** *Goats love to nibble the leaves, twigs, and bark on branches. Cut some off the trees and give them to your goats for a treat.*

eaten are also significant. Feed intake fluctuates with temperature, and a goat's appetite is subject to thermo-regulatory control. The amount of time spent eating and the rate of mastication both tend to increase as the temperature goes down.

However, when the temperature drops below 50°F (10°C), eating activity decreases again. There is a correlation between lower temperatures and reduced water intake, and restricting the amount of water consumed will reduce a goat's dry food consumption.

Goats can distinguish between bitter, salty, sweet, and sour tastes. They have a higher tolerance than most animals to bitter tasting feeds, which might explain their browsing predilection for bark, leaves, shoots, shrubs, and branches.

They tend to spend more time eating each day than other ruminants, often for as long as eleven hours. This may be misleading because they also spend more time moving from one plant to another than sheep or cattle. The length and the regularity of rumination is inversely related to the goat's alertness, with long regular periods of rumination occurring during a semi-drowsy state. If they're subjected to random noises, rumination may become irregular and fully alert goats will generally not ruminate.

### Goats on pasture

Letting your goats graze freely on pasture has the advantage of providing them with easy access to shade and water. However, it

## GOAT FACT

In an unconfined grazing system, goats will almost uniformly reject any plants contaminated with the scent of their own species' urine or feces. From an evolutionary standpoint, this is significant in that it limits parasite infestation.

is important to rotate the animals among pastures where possible. This permits the pasture to rejuvenate and also tends to break the cycle of internal parasites. You should always have salt and a mineral mix available in the goathouse or offer a mix of equal parts trace mineral salt and dicalcium phosphate. Even if the goats graze freely on pasture, you must also provide ready access to hay. And remember that during early spring you should be alert to possible cases of bloat and grass tetani.

## FEEDING GOATS

Although goats get many nutrients from grazing, especially in April, May, and June, you must provide good-quality hay all year round as it is high in fiber, which is vital for the efficient functioning of the goat's rumen (fore-stomach). If you have pregnant females, kids, milking goats, or working males, you should also feed concentrated feed to provide energy and proteins. You can buy a specially formulated goat mix from many feed merchants. Sugar beet pulp, lucerne nuts, clean greens, and roots will also be appreciated by your goats.

The quantity you feed will depend on the goat's size, general condition and productivity. For example, a growing dairy goat may need about 1 lb (500 g) of concentrated feed a day, whereas a milker may need almost 4 lb (2 kg). You should also provide a mineral lick and make it available to your goats at all times.

**Hay**

From May until August, nonproductive free-range goats need only have hay on wet days or at night. However, good-quality hay should always be provided for the rest of the year. A visual examination of hay can yield considerable information about its quality. For example:

■ An earlier cutting date indicates more digestible nutrients.

■ More leaves provide more protein and minerals for your goats.

■ A lack of seed heads indicates early cutting of the hay.

■ Coarse stems suggest late cutting while crushed stems indicate early removal from the field and, thus, less damage.

■ Foreign material (weeds or tree leaves) mean reduced feed value.

■ A green color indicates the presence of vitamin A.

## WATER INTAKE

Goats are well adapted to limited water intake and short-term shortages, as their water turnover rate is only 85cc/lb (188 cc/kg) in twenty-four hours. This compares well with 84 cc/lb (185 cc/kg) in twenty-four hours for the camel, an animal renowned for its ability to go without water for long periods of time. During colder months, when sweating or respiratory cooling is not necessary for maintaining of body temperature, goats can often sustain an adequate intake of water from their grazed feeds alone.

During environmental temperatures of about 100°F (38°C), the panting rate of respiratory cooling is about half that of sheep. Their sweating is limited, and the

## HAY HARVESTING

The date of the harvest is the most important single factor that affects feed consumption and quality. As the stage of maturity changes, there is a marked effect on the protein content of the hay. As the protein content decreases over this period, the fiber content increases from about twenty-seven to thirty-eight percent. When this occurs, the digestible energy values not only decline but the crop is less palatable so that the goats consume less.

loss of water through feces and urine is much reduced. Reduced water intake over a period of several days will result in a corresponding decrease in the excretion of urine, with the concentration of urea being increased.

Water intake will be much greater for lactating goats. This is because milk is approximately eighty percent water. The greater the milk production of the goat, the more water it will require. You should provide plenty of clean drinking water for your goats at all times, and drinking troughs and buckets must always be kept clean.

## HOUSING

Goats are generally hardy animals, being able to weather the heat and the cold comparatively well as long as they are provided with a well-constructed shed. But they dislike wind and rain and will run to the nearest available shelter on the approach of a storm, often arriving before the first drops of rain have fallen. They

**Below:** *A custom-made wooden goathouse with plenty of dry straw on the floor for bedding down is perfect for raising goats.*

also have an intense aversion to water puddles and mud. They can soon get soaked to the skin as they have very little oil in their coats, and this can lead to disease or even pneumonia.

While hot weather poses no great problems to most goats, high humidity does cause them stress. This will lower the milk production, cause loss of body weight, and may even incite antisocial behavior in some goats.

Goats do not need fancy housing but they must have access to adequate shelter at all times, especially dairy goats, which should be housed at night throughout the year as well as in bad weather. Many older buildings can be adapted to cut costs. The usual type of housing is the shed-type, which will provide adequate shelter and allow access to grazing. The advantage of this type of housing is that you can keep building, construction and maintenance costs to the minimum.

The building can be constructed from wood, brick, stone or concrete blocks. Avoid corrugated iron, which is not very warm. Above all, the goats should be kept dry and free from drafts. Adjoining the building, it is a good idea to have a concreted exercise yard. Goats are herd animals and like company and usually they are penned together. However, you can divide the housing and yard into separate pens of at least 25 square feet (2.3 square meters). Internal pens can be made with metal hurdles or wood but make sure that there are no sharp edges

**Above:** *You should provide a hay rack and mineral lick on the wall of the goathouse for your goats to enjoy as they wish.*

or projections that could injure your goats. Also ensure that horned and hornless goats are never penned together or they could suffer injuries.

The floor inside the goathouse can be dirt rather than concrete but a solid floor that can be washed down is better. You should provide at least 15 square feet (1.4 square meters) of bedded area for each goat. The floor should be bedded regularly with dry straw to absorb any moisture. Dirty soiled bedding should be removed frequently to keep the area clean.

Goat management will be easier for you if there is plenty of light inside the building. However, cover windows with weldmesh rather than glass to provide adequate ventilation for the goats. If there are electric light fittings or wires, ensure that they are out of the animals' reach.

You will also need to provide a metal or wooden hayrack with a lid. You can make one yourself or buy one ready-made. Position it at head height for the goats – it should be high enough for them to reach in comfort but not so low that it can be soiled. For storing hay, straw, and feed, you will need a clean, dry area that is protected from predators and vermin.

**Below:** *Anglo-Nubian goats are instantly recognizable with their Roman noses and pendulous bell-shaped ears.*

If you intend to milk your goats, you will need a separate milking parlor and this must be kept scrupulously clean.

## OUTSIDE EXERCISE AREAS

Goats prefer to be outside on fine days, even when it is cold. The outside exercise area should provide a minimum of 25 square feet (2.3 square meters) of space per animal (see opposite) and should be well-drained and properly fenced. Goats like to lean on fences to greet visitors. A 6-in (15-cm) woven wire fence that is 4–5 feet (1.5 meters) high is adequate. Place an overhanging wire about 10–12 in (25–30 cm) from the inside and top of the fence, supported by offset pieces nailed to the posts. Put snap hooks on all gates as goats are adept at unlatching them.

## GOAT MANAGEMENT

Goats can be kept free-range in a house and a yard, or tethered (although this is not recommended).

■ **Free-range goats** have access to grazing and are housed at night-time, in wet weather, and sometimes during the cold winter months. The most fortunate free-range goats have unrestricted access to grassland but this must be securely fenced and have a field shelter.

■ **Yarded goats** are kept in a house and yard, making goat management easier in some respects as they are confined to a relatively small area. However, you will have to provide them with good-quality plant food and greenstuff, cut grass, and branches, as they cannot browse freely on pasture.

■ **Tethered goats** have to be moved constantly to fresh grazing. This is time-consuming for you and is a problem in hot, wet, or cold weather when the animals need shelter and protection from wind, rain, and hot sun. The grazing must be suitable and regular supervision is essential to prevent the goats becoming entangled in the ropes, which can lead to strangulation, so you should not keep goats if you only intend to tether them.

## DAIRY GOATS

If you plan to keep dairy goats, you will be taking on the responsibility of milking them twice a day, seven days a week. If you are not prepared to do this, then you should not consider a dairy breed. Milk yields vary according to the breed and you may well have a surplus of milk. If you are planning to sell the milk or milk products, you must follow the regulations and strict requirements that are laid down by law. For more information, you should consult the USDA and/or the Food and Drug Administration.

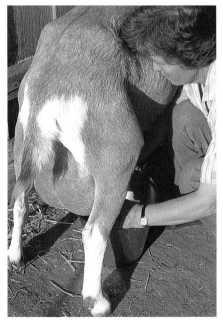

**Above:** *Milking is easy and doesn't take long although good milkers, such as Toggenburgs and Alpines, need twice-daily milking.*

# Goat behavior

## SEXUALITY

Sexual behavior among most goats originating in the temperate zones is seasonal, with the females lacking an estrus period during the late spring and summer months. The sex drive of the buck is also at a low ebb during this time. The volume and motility of semen is greatest during the late summer and autumn.

The return to normal sexual behavior is first achieved by the buck, generally about two weeks before the doe returns to estrus. It is thought that the courting of the buck may accelerate the onset of the breeding season. The length of the season is influenced by the number of hours of daylight, the temperature, and geographical origin.

## SELF-PRESERVATION

When alarmed, goats will stamp one forefoot and produce a high-pitched, sneezing sound. Goat herds exhibit a tendency to move a short distance away, forming a thin line in front of any disturbance. If pursued, the group will tend to disperse. This prevents them from being herded like sheep, which tend to bunch together while being pursued. Young kids, instead of following their mothers, freeze at the first sign of any danger. By standing stock still, a predator may sometimes pass them by.

**Below:** *Goats soon get used to other animals, but care is needed with dogs.*

# What do I get?

## GOAT'S MILK

The upsurge of interest in the "poor man's cow" has much to do with an increasing desire to attain some measure of self-sufficiency and to gain a better control over food sources. A goat makes sense: she will eat little, occupy a small area, and produce sufficient milk for the average family.

Indeed, a good milker will yield about a gallon of milk a day. Weigh in the balance the practicalities of maintaining a cow in a suburban backyard and the

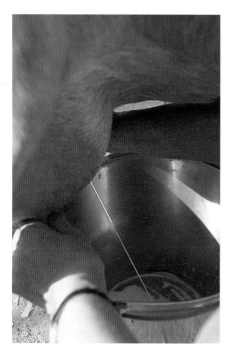

scheme withers on the vine. Substitute a goat for a cow in the equation and the idea becomes achievable.

### The taste of goat's milk

As interest in the dairy goat grows, the many and various misconceptions, discrepancies, and exaggerated claims surrounding her milk tend to multiply. Foremost in this list is the general complaint that goat's milk has a peculiar odor or taste to it. Occasionally this may be the case but it is untrue more often than not. The taint to milk and therefore to further processed products can often be traced back to the presence of the buck and failing to observe the most basic rule of never allowing him to get near or even downwind of the dairy herd at milking time.

### Milking your goats

Goats require milking twice a day, seven days a week. They produce the highest yields between four and twelve weeks after kidding. Milk production in winter is about half that of summer. Most goats will "run through" or give milk, but in smaller quantities, in the second year after kidding.

**Left:** *When milking your goats, position a clean pail or container under the udder to collect the milk.*

## MILKING GUIDELINES

In order to produce clean, nutritious milk, you must comply with the following:
- Your goats must be healthy, free of disease, and in good condition.
- You must keep the milking area clean and dust-free, with no flies.
- You must wash down the floor and walls of the milking area after milking.
- You must wear a clean overall and wash your hands before milking each goat.
- You must keep the hair on the goat's udder, flanks, and hind legs clipped and short.
- You should wash and dry the goat's udder and teats.
- You should examine the fore-milk (the first two or three squirts of milk) for clots or flakes before proceeding with the milking.
- You must strain the milk immediately through a filter into the milk churn.
- You must cool the milk to 43°F (6°C) as soon as possible after milking.

### Composition and allergies

Goat's milk is similar to cow's milk in its basic composition of dry matter, protein, fat, lactose, and minerals, but it is in the area of effect on the digestive system that gaps begin to appear. Allergic reactions, especially in very young children, don't seem to be triggered by goat's milk.

## CHEESE-MAKING

When cheese is made, the milk solids are separated from the whey. In order for this to happen, the protein (casein) in the milk must be either coagulated or clotted, either by adding rennet or through the presence of acid in the milk. After the milk has been coagulated, you can treat the curd in a number of ways to produce different types of cheeses.

You may use fresh or frozen goat's milk but it should not be heated before making into cheese. After milking, the milk should be strained, cooled, and refrigerated at a temperature below 43°F (6°C) before you use it for cheese-making.

You do not need to invest in any expensive equipment. All you need for making the most basic soft cheese are a saucepan, a thermometer, some cheesecloth or muslin, and a bowl. If you are embarking on more adventurous cheeses, you may also need a cheese vat, mats and boards, a draining rack, and molds.

### Making high-quality cheese

You must have high-quality milk to make high-quality cheese.
- It must be free from unpleasant flavors or they will be intensified in the cheese.
- It must be free from foreign bodies, including traces of antibiotics.
- It should contain relatively few non-pathogenic bacteria.

If you are making cheese at home for your own personal consumption, then obviously you need not be greatly concerned about composition but if you are planning to sell the cheese, it will have to meet certain FDA standards.

### Making soft cheese

This is the easiest cheese of all to make and ideal for beginners.

**1** Heat 1 gallon (5 liters) of clean milk to a temperature of 80°F (27°C) and let stand for 36–48 hours at a temperature of 75–85°F (24–30°C). This sours the milk and aids the formation of a firm curd.

**2** Put the curd into a piece of muslin or cheesecloth and leave to drain. You can hang the bag of curd above a bowl or place it in a metal strainer. Open the cloth occasionally and scrape the sides down with a clean spoon to speed up the drainage.

**3** Place the bag of curd on a metal grid and weight it down with a 1 lb (500 g) weight. Leave to stand for several hours in a cool place.

**4** Remove the cheese from the bag and season to taste with salt. If you wish, mix in some chopped herbs of your choice, or even ground spices, depending on the flavor you want.

## PASTEURIZING GOAT'S MILK

If you are nervous about using fresh milk for cheese-making, or are unsure about its quality, then it's always a good idea to pasteurize the milk first. This mild heat treatment will destroy some pathogenic bacteria and milk spoilage organisms. Pasteurized milk can be kept longer than nonpasteurized.

**1** Heat the milk to 145°F (63°C) and keep it at this temperature for 30 minutes, stirring occasionally.

**2** Allow the milk to cool to less than 10°C (42°F), stirring occasionally.

## YOGURT-MAKING

You can make yogurt by introducing specific bacteria to the goat's milk and thereby changing its physical and chemical content. You should use only the highest-quality fresh milk, which has high protein and butterfat percentages, or the yogurt may not set properly. Never be tempted to use old or off-flavored milk or cream on the basis that the end-product will have a sour flavor anyway.

To make good-quality yogurt, you need a starter culture. As a beginner, it may be better to buy this.

**1** Heat 18 fl oz (500 ml ) full-cream milk to 180°F (82°C). Keep the milk at this temperature for 30 minutes, then cool to 110°F (43°C). You can use a thermometer to check the temperatures, or you can buy a commercial yogurt maker to do it for you.

**2** Add 1 teaspoon (5 ml) starter culture to the milk and stir gently.

**3** Pour into glass pots in an electric yogurt maker, or into a thermos flask, and leave to incubate overnight. The yogurt can then be refrigerated until you are ready to eat it.

# What to expect

## KIDDING

Kidding is an essential part of goat management and, with the possible exception of the nutritional needs of the doe, has the greatest effect on milk production. Breeding is possible at seven months or less, there is a short gestation interval of 150 days and two or more offspring per pregnancy.

Your goatkeeping skills will be put to the test to look after the nutritional needs of the gestating doe in late lactation and during the dry period. With so short a pregnancy, most of the development of the fetus occurs when the nutritional demands on the doe are at their lowest. She will need adequate food to produce healthy kids. Depending on her size and the forage source, feed her 1½ lb (675 g) of twelve percent concentrate daily.

She should also get plenty of exercise and always have access to clean, cool water and trace-mineral salts, together with a supplement of bone meal. Although feeding calcium will aid fetal development, don't overdo it.

**Below:** *The kids are born in the spring; most does usually give birth to two offspring.*

## Birth

The kids should be born in a clean environment; either a well-rotated pasture or a stall well bedded with straw or some other absorbent material. Each kid has developed in a germ-free environment and delivery represents its first exposure to the possibility of disease.

The location of the kidding stall or pasture should be near at hand so that you can keep an eye on the doe in case there are kidding difficulties. Few adult does require assistance when the time comes but first-timers should be closely watched, especially if bred to bucks, which are known to sire large offspring.

At birth, you should dip the umbilical cord in a solution of tincture of iodine as a preventative measure against bacteria. Cut the umbilical cord to 3–4 inches (7.5–10 cm) in length. A bleeding cord should be tied with surgical suture material. Dipping the cord in iodine not only prevents entry of organisms but promotes rapid drying and the eventual breaking away. If you are worried, ask your vet for advice.

The kids should be bottle-fed some colostrum milk as soon after birth as possible because it contains antibodies. Any excess milk can be frozen for use with orphan or bonus kids.

**Below:** *Kids only consume small amounts of milk when they suckle, and they may often need bottle-feeding as well.*

## Feeding the young kids

Milk is the principal component of the diet of the pre-weaning kid. There are numerous ways to feed milk, including:

- Bottles or pails
- Suckling the dam
- Nursing does.

With any system, the health of the kid, sanitation and hygiene, and how much time you have to spare are the major factors to consider.

Under natural suckling, kids consume small amounts of milk at very frequent intervals. Bottle-feeding is more labor-intensive but the kids will receive more individual attention and are easier to handle later on.

Increase in size and weight are not the only measures of success in weaning. A well-formed skeleton and the proper development of internal organs are often neglected if the emphasis is on rapid weight gain. You should aim for an average daily weight gain of about 9 oz (250 g) during the first few weeks.

## Introducing dry feeds

By limiting the daily milk intake to about 4 pints (2.2 liters), you can speed up the introduction of dry foods. These are important for developing body capacity.

Kids should be eating pasture grass or hay by two weeks of age, and grain within four weeks. Pay particular consideration to concentrate supplements. Palatability is the key, and thus molasses, chopped or rolled corn, and whole or rolled oats all make good ingredients. Strike a balance of protein by adding some soybean meal.

## Weaning the kids

Several factors influence when the kids should be weaned. The most important consideration is whether or not their average daily consumption of concentrate and forage is adequate for growth and development to continue in the absence of milk. Basically there is no fixed age at which weaning should begin. However, as a guide, it should be when the kids are two or two-and-a-half times their birth weight. Milk feeding may promote rapid growth but keeping the kids on a milk-only diet can delay further development and predispose them to diarrhea.

## Feeding the growing kids

Forage will make up the bulk of their diet. Mix in concentrates or simple grains to provide the nutrients that cannot be derived from grazing. The leaves and young stems chosen during browsing have crude protein and digestible energy values higher than the average for the whole plant. If you're going to formulate a supplementation program for your kids' forage-based diet, you must try to estimate what the kids are actually consuming rather than what is available.

## Looking after the weaned kids

Exercise, fresh water, and access to salt and minerals are all important in the post-weaning period. You must pay

special attention to controlling internal parasites, especially coccidiosis. Ask your veterinarian to recommend the appropriate treatment. Trim the hooves frequently to ensure that their feet develop properly.

### Dehorning kids

Kids should be dehorned between three and seven days of age, while the horn bud is visible. The hair should be clipped and a hot electric disbudder held over the area for fifteen to twenty seconds with firm even pressure. The center of the ring formed by the iron should also be burned and the cap remaining taken off. You can use a local anesthetic to reduce any pain and permit easier handling of the kid but if dehorning is done before seven days, it should be relatively painless.

**Above:** *If you decide not to dehorn the kids, you must keep them penned separately from kids or goats without horns to prevent injuries.*

### Castration of males

Castration of male kids can be undertaken on the second day after birth. You can either have a veterinarian do this surgically or you can do this yourself. The best method is to use a rubber ring, which you can borrow from your vet. Slip it over the testicles and release the elastrator. The testicles will drop off and the kid will feel no pain.

### Teeth

Milk teeth are present either at birth or shortly afterward and will remain for about a year before they are replaced with the permanent adult teeth.

# Healthcare

## GOAT DISEASES

Goat diseases are like those of cattle and sheep living in similar regions. They tend to have more internal parasites, but have less tuberculosis, milk fever, post partum ketosis, and brucellosis. Find an experienced small ruminant veterinarian *before* you need one.

### Vaccinations
You should get your goat vaccinated against tetanus and enterotoxemia (similar to pulpy kidney). Ask your veterinarian for advice.

### Internal parasites
All goats are hosts to internal parasites, especially tapeworm, roundworm, and liver fluke, and they must be kept under control by a worming program. If they are left untreated, they will quickly multiply and the goat will get thinner as it will not be able to absorb the goodness in its feed. A severe parasite infestation may eventually cause anemia or even death. Ask your vet to provide the necessary drugs so that you can de-worm your goat regularly. Kids, too, will need to be wormed from the age of two months.

### External parasites
Even the best-kept goats are affected by lice at some time. If your goats are starting to nibble themselves, use a specially formulated delousing treatment. Mites can cause mange and bald patches; ask your veterinarian for advice.

## FOOT CARE

Goats' feet grow very quickly and need trimming once a month. This prevents foot rot and lameness. Start trimming the feet when your goat is young.
**1** Tie her up against a wall in a comfortable position.
**2** Lift one foot and, holding it firmly in one hand, or between your legs, pare off the outside overgrown wall of the hoof with a sharp knife.
**3** Stop trimming when the pink sole starts to appear.

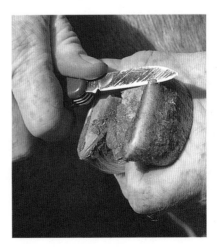

# CHAPTER FIVE

# Beekeeping

People throughout the world have been using honey as a source of sweetness for thousands of years but, unlike other species valued as a food source, the honeybee has never been tamed. We have domesticated many wild creatures over time but our relationship with the honeybee has progressed to that of landlord and tenant rather than master and slave. What has always attracted us to these fascinating creatures is the fruits of their labor.

# Introduction

It is unlikely that *Apis mellifera* would ever have been raised in our affections much above her near relatives, the wasp and the ant, had it not been for the importance of honey and wax. But there has always been a price for us to pay and it is worth mentioning two purely physical considerations before deciding whether or not to enter the ranks of apiarists, namely, the bee's sting and your strength.

## COPING WITH STINGS

If you are stung by a honeybee, scrape the sting free from the wound with a fingernail as quickly as possible. This will reduce the amount of venom injected and the consequent irritation. Because the poison sac of the honeybee's sting is attached to it, any attempt to grasp the sting to pull it out will only result in squeezing more poison into the wound.

## BEE STINGS

There is no escaping the fact that working so closely with bees you will be stung at some point and that it will hurt. How much it hurts depends on you as an individual, and most of us can tolerate the brief discomfort. However, for a tiny minority of us there is the danger of a fatal anaphylactic shock. Most people will already know their susceptibility to bee venom but it is worth finding out for sure before putting your hand in a hive and it is also worth checking out other members of your immediate family.

## STRENGTH AND PHYSICAL LABOR

The second point to emphasize is that beekeeping requires a certain amount of physical exertion. Anybody with a weak back is likely to find the condition exacerbated by the manipulation of hives and the carrying of heavy loads.

## DO SOME RESEARCH

Finally, it is a good idea to introduce yourself to the reality of beekeeping before going too far down the road. There are no theoretical reasons to preclude anybody from entering apiculture, but a first acquaintance with a noisy thriving

colony of honeybees can be daunting and is best experienced in the company of someone who has seen it all before. Almost without exception, experienced beekeepers are enthusiasts and are happy to share their passion with an interested novice. Arrange to visit a beekeeper so you can see him at work and find out what is involved. It's important to any

**Above:** *The beekeeper must always wear a protective veil and clothing when opening up the hive for routine examinations.*

future relationship that you should be happy to proceed, having seen, smelled, and heard a colony at close quarters. Join your local beekeeping association and attend their meetings.

# What do I want?

There is no point in keeping bees if you dislike the idea of plenty of honey or the company of low-flying workaholics. It is inevitable that you will produce a surplus of honey and will have to find some use for it. You may also find that your neighbors won't welcome a sudden increase in the local population of bees. Forming an idea of your aims before being confronted by a small mountain of beeswax would be a useful exercise, although the equipment manufacturers or their agents will buy any surplus clean wax.

## LOCATING THE BEES

It is also quite important to the well-being of your bees that the location you have in mind for them will sustain them. Honey reflects the source of the nectar, and although it is composed of fructose, glucose, and water in varying proportions, its color and flavor depend on its floral origins.

It is a myth to think that you have to live in the countryside in order to keep bees. Bees are kept successfully in suburban and even in urban areas. There are numerous flowers in parks, gardens, and overgrown lots. The only real disadvantage to a city or town location for a bee colony is the increased risk of nuisance complaints.

## THE ATTRACTION OF BEEKEEPING

Most people like honey but not everyone likes honeybees. Most of us are happy to buy rather than to produce the honey we eat and, although our interest in where products come from is increasing, it remains true to say that we don't really "understand" much of what we consume.

One of the greatest attractions to beekeeping is that it places a microcosm in our own backyard, fostering a practical interest in the interplay between man-made and natural phenomena and demonstrating quite forcibly how they impact on each other.

**Above:** *These are examples of hives found in Great Britain.*

# Who's who in the hive

There is only one species of honeybee of interest to European or North American beekeepers, *Apis mellifera*. There are several races within this group that are distinguished by, among other things, the following:

- Color
- Resilience to disease
- Ruggedness
- Productivity
- Swarming tendencies
- Overall temperament.

**Honeybee colonies**

All honeybees belong to the order Hymenoptera, which includes other bees, wasps, and ants. Most Hymenoptera have two pairs of clear wings, all have chewing mouthparts, and some, including the honeybee, can suck up liquids. These small insects undergo a four-stage developmental metamorphosis passing from egg through larva and pupa into adulthood.

Honeybees are supremely well adapted to collect pollen and nectar. They are covered with finely branched hairs that trap pollen as they visit flowers in bloom. While visiting, they gather pollen from these hairs and store it in "pollen baskets" on their hind legs. The proboscis sucks up nectar.

Honeybees under management are driven by the same instincts as their wild counterparts, and the key objective of the successful beekeeper is to anticipate and harness this natural behavior.

The first point to be made about honeybees is that they are highly social insects, living cheek by jowl in extremely well organized colonies. Each member of the group has a specific job to do and no bee can develop or survive in isolation. The three distinct kinds of honeybees in a colony are as follows:

- The queen
- The workers
- The drones.

Let's consider them one by one, starting at the top of the hierarchy.

## THE QUEEN

The queen is the mother of all the other bees in the hive and the biggest. She is distinguished by having the longest abdomen and the broadest thorax and brighter colored legs. Her wings appear short in proportion to the rest of her but are, in fact, slightly longer than those of the worker. Her most important task is to lay eggs. Her productivity depends on the amount of food the workers bring in and the amount of brood space in the colony. She can lay more than 1,900 eggs a day, laying a solid pattern of brood, meaning one egg in every cell.

A good healthy queen will make the best use of available space; a few eggs

**Above:** *The queen can be identified by the distinctive white spot on her back. The queen is marked in this way so that she can be located easily among a mass of other bees.*

scattered among many empty cells, or several eggs per cell, are the first signs of problems to come and should be investigated sooner rather than later.

### New queens

Worker bees usually rear new queens for one of the following reasons:

■ The colony of bees decides to swarm and the old queen will depart before a new one emerges

■ The queen is laying a decreasing number of eggs as a result of old age

■ Accidental loss of the queen.

The sudden accidental loss of its queen will confuse and agitate a colony but it will fast begin to repair the gap by rearing a new one. Worker eggs or larvae, if they are less than three days old, are raised in hastily constructed queen cells that hang vertically and are about the size and shape of the shell of a peanut. A fertilized egg hatches in roughly three days and the developing larva is nourished by a special food called "royal jelly." After growing rapidly for about six days, the larva pupates in the cell and the new queen emerges in approximately eight days.

The newly emerged queen goes on the warpath immediately by fighting any rivals she finds, and the colony usually destroys the extra queen cells. Between six to eight days after emerging, the queen seeks male company for the only time, mating high in the air with several drones. She then settles down to the main business of laying eggs, having achieved a sufficient store of sperm to last her lifetime. She will leave the hive only with a swarm, which is nature's way of establishing colonies at new locations.

**Failing queens**

Queens can live up to five years but egg production declines significantly after two years, and although some beekeepers retain a queen beyond her prime, most replace her every second year to keep the colony vigorous and to lessen the danger of swarming, which often occurs just prior to the main nectar flow – colonies that swarm have drastically reduced honey production. A queen may begin to fail at any time, and will display several tell-tale symptoms:

■ An old queen usually has a dark, dull appearance because her body hairs have broken or rubbed off

■ The edges of her wings might have become worn and ragged

■ Her abdomen might droop from her thorax

■ She may move more slowly and begin trying to avoid the worker bees.

## REQUEENING

You can produce queen cells simply by removing the queen, creating an emergency status, and within a day or so, between five and fifteen emergency cells will have been started. After these cells are capped, they can be cut out and transferred to another colony. After emerging and mating, the colony is thus requeened with a queen of your choosing. This is a simple way of producing queens but will not give the best results. Proper queen breeding is complicated and is best left to experienced beekeepers.

■ A consequence of advancing age is that she will lay only drone eggs.

The brood area of a failing queen is smaller than normal and you will notice that honey production is on the decrease even when conditions appear favorable. Sensing something amiss, the workers begin building supersedure cells near the center of the comb in preparation for replacing her. At this point, it could be said to be just as well to let the queen be superseded rather than to introduce a new one artificially.

Requeening is best done in the autumn. The colony is not too large at this time, and a good queen will be in place for the build-up to spring.

## THE WORKERS

Workers are not as big as either the queen or drone but they far outnumber both. There might be only a few thousand during the winter and early spring but there are usually many thousands during the summer when pollen and nectar are abundant. A thriving colony at full strength can have up to 100,000 workers, and their labor powers the intricate hierarchy of the hive.

A worker's life begins as a fertilized egg. Laid singly in cells, each egg is attached to the bottom of the cell and stands upright, hatching out in about three days. Each larva is initially fed on royal jelly for three days, the composition of which is changed for the subsequent period.

The white grub-like larva moults five times during the six days and, just before maturity, house bees cap the cell. The larva then spins a cocoon and becomes a pupa. The adult emerges twelve days later. It takes about twenty-one days to mature from the egg to an adult bee ready for work.

### Job descriptions

The tasks of the workers change with age. House bees, as they are known, look after the indoor work. The tasks they are called upon to do are timetabled to match their abilities and strength.

▪ **Days 1–3:** The newly emerged bee is cleaning cells.

**Below:** *These worker bees are working away busily on the comb inside the hive.*

■ **Days 4–9:** It is busy in the nursery making brood food from the glands in its head and feeding it to the younger larvae.

■ **Day 9 onward:** The wax glands on its abdomen begin functioning and it is then kept busy forming it into combs (cell structures containing honey and brood).

■ **Days 17–19:** It accepts pollen and nectar from the field bees, placing it in cells. It also helps to evaporate excess water from the nectar and to turn it into honey, and packs the pollen down into the cells for storage – this is commonly known as bee bread.

■ **Day 20 onward:** It may act as a guard against intruders before eventually taking on the most arduous phase of its life in the fields as a forager.

All worker bees fan their wings for ventilation in the summer, controlling

**Above:** *These workers are passing nectar to each other as they work on the comb. A full-strength colony may have 100,000 workers.*

**Above:** *This worker bee is unloading some pollen into the cells in the comb.*

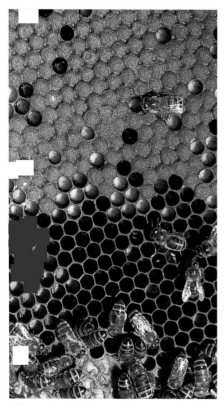

**Above:** *In this photograph, you can clearly see the larvae and the sealed brood. The little white dots are the larvae.*

temperature and humidity, and they will also generate heat in wintertime. But their gathering of nectar, pollen, and water is perhaps their most important function and, considering the hectic nature of their daily round, it comes as no surprise that the average adult worker's lifespan is five to six weeks during the busy season. Overwintering bees are perhaps luckier and will survive for several months.

## THE DRONES

Drones are bigger than workers but not as long as queens. They have large eyes that meet each other at the top of the head and they do not have stings, pollen baskets on their legs, or glands for producing wax. Their mouthparts are too short to gather nectar and they do no jobs around the hive. Their only function is to fertilize the queen, and they die in the process. As if this wasn't bad enough, any survivors are banished from the hive before winter begins.

Queens and workers develop from fertilized eggs but drones develop from unfertilized eggs. Their cells are slightly larger than worker cells, which seems to stimulate the queen to lay only the unfertilized eggs in them. Small drones can develop in worker cells if an aging queen loses her ability to fertilize eggs. It takes a drone twenty-four days to develop from egg to adulthood.

## THE COLONY

Honeybee colonies can be likened to a single animal. Individual bees are the cells and tissues. When one part is threatened, the whole colony reacts. If an essential part becomes diseased or is destroyed, the colony can often heal itself and it may also divide and become two or more separate entities. The colony also adapts to survive different seasons.

During the late autumn, only small

quantities of nectar and pollen are introduced into the colony. As often as not there is no brood being reared at this time and so the colony will not grow. Early autumn nectar flows usually allow a sufficient number of young bees to be reared to survive the winter.

The colony needs honey for energy, and pollen for protein, minerals and vitamins to survive the winter and raise brood in early spring. Its survival depends on a good cluster of young bees and an adequate food supply. If the cluster is too small, it cannot generate enough heat to survive and the bees die if their corporate body temperature drops much below 93–95°F (34–35°C). The colony must be able to make and save heat to survive the rigors of winter.

Bees produce heat by digesting honey and conserve it by bunching tightly together in a group. The outer layer of bees is an insulating shell that traps the heat in the center of the cluster. The bees on the outer layers periodically change places so that none of them becomes too cold and the cluster expands or contracts according to the ambient temperature outside the hive.

Bees are inactive in the hive if the thermometer falls below 57°F (14°C) and they won't even move to get honey that is not adjacent to the cluster. If it stays cold for too many consecutive days, bees can starve even if honey is just a few inches away. The colony soon runs out of heat and freezes.

## SELECTIVE BREEDING

A race of bees is not like a breed of dog. The former have not been tightly controlled and, unlike breeders of domesticated livestock, beekeepers haven't employed significant genetic selection techniques because bee reproduction itself wasn't understood until 1845. Because the queen bee mates with several drones away from the hive, selection of the male line is difficult and in most places impossible. Artificial insemination is practiced but this is not for the beginner.

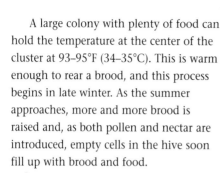

A large colony with plenty of food can hold the temperature at the center of the cluster at 93–95°F (34–35°C). This is warm enough to rear a brood, and this process begins in late winter. As the summer approaches, more and more brood is raised and, as both pollen and nectar are introduced, empty cells in the hive soon fill up with brood and food.

Bees need to live in colonies but they dislike cramped conditions. If there is not enough room to expand the brood area and store honey, a section of the colony will leave in a swarm. Overcrowded bees are likely to swarm whereas those with plenty of living room are generally happy to stay put in the hive and the colony will continue to develop.

**Below:** *These worker bees are clustered together on the sealed brood cells. The process of rearing brood begins in late winter.*

# What they need

## BEE HIVES

There is more than one type of hive available, but some of these are too small for strong colonies. It is best to start with the right type of equipment as changing it later is very difficult. Beware that you do not acquire equipment that has been discarded by other beekeepers as useless or unsuitable. There is no point in buying rotten wood or a type of hive that has long since been superseded by a better design.

### Hive treatment

Since the inside surfaces of the bee hive should not be painted, the coating on the outer surface is stressed by water migrating from the inside of the hive. Oil-based paints are the worst and will readily peel.

Due to ease of application and lower cost, latex paints were common choices.

**Above:** *This National hive is commonly used by many beekeepers in Great Britain. All hives can be easily disassembled by the working beekeeper.*

The rubber-based latex paints will flex and resist peeling better. In recent years, polyurethane exterior stains have become

## EQUIPMENT YOU WILL NEED

As a general guide, the beginner will need the following equipment: a bee veil, a pair of bee gloves, a smoker, and a hive tool. It is best to purchase bees as a complete colony in a hive or as a nucleus that can be put into a hive in the spring to develop as the season progresses. If you have a complete empty hive, you may be able to obtain a swarm but this means the bees are of uncertain origin and it may contain diseases.

You will also need extra honey supers and, if possible, an additional empty hive with frames. The secretary of your local beekeepers association will be able to advise you where to obtain the bees and equipment.

**Above:** *This hive has been disassembled and the roof removed so that the various layers inside are clearly visible, including the queen excluder and frames.*

**Left:** *A complete hive with supers. You can buy empty hives with frames; ask your local beekeepers association for advice.*

popular; many of these stains are water repellent and resist mildew and fading.

■ **Warning:** Pressure-treated wood is now in universal use. However, the materials that are used to preserve the wood are usually toxic to honeybees and so their use in hive construction is not to be recommended.

### Comb honey

Before the extractor came into common use, comb honey was the norm rather than the exception. Over the years, many different designs have been tried to facilitate the production, harvesting, and sale of comb honey. An efficient means was eventually discovered using squares made from thin sheets of basswood. Because of the long grain in this wood, it could be scored and folded to form the standard 12-oz (350-g) section. A more recent method is to use round plastic containers for sections.

The more common way is to use unwired foundation in super frames and then cut the sealed comb in six parts, giving 225-g (8-oz) cut comb, which can be put in special containers.

### Using plastics

Plastic equipment is in use in some aspects of apiculture, including hive components. It is also widely used in wax foundation bases and frames. Plastic frames resist wax moth damage but they have a tendency to warp when exposed to sunlight and are difficult to sterilize with heat.

**Above:** *In this frame, the honey has been sealed within the comb and capped with wax ready for extraction by the beekeeper.*

## LITTLE USED BUT FAR FROM USELESS

■ **A division board** is used to take the place of a frame in the brood box when a population is small.

■ **An entrance block** can be used to protect small colonies.

■ **Hive-top feeders** work well because it is unnecessary to open the colony to refill and they hold more than bucket feeders.

■ **A ventilated bottom board** increases airflow during summer and winter.

■ **Painting various patterns** on the front of hives can help bees identify their own hive.

■ **Two colonies can be united** by placing a sheet of newspaper between them. The queenless brood box is normally put on top. Place newspaper over a queen excluder so that it does not stick to the frames.

## HIVE LOCATION

Bees can fly for more than two miles in search of pollen and nectar but they do better the less ground they have to cover. They can be kept pretty well anywhere but choosing the optimum location will make their life easier and will increase the chance of a strong and productive colony. To this end, you should always bear the following points in mind when selecting a suitable site for the hive.

### Water supply

Bees always need a ready supply of water to dilute the honey for their own consumption and to aid the cooling of the hive in hot weather. If there is a nearby pond, so much the better and they can then concentrate their time and energy gathering nectar rather than fetching and carrying water. A dripping garden hose or water trough filled with coarse gravel can be sited close by but it is worthy of note that bees can easily drown in deep open water.

### Temperature

Bee behavior is sensitive to changes in temperature. They rarely work when the thermometer is below 55°F (13°C) or is higher than 100°F (38°C) and they cannot fly at all if it dips below 50°F (10°C). On very hot days, they will cluster outside unshaded hives and will do no work. Windbreaks provide some protection against cold winter chills as bees eat more

from their larder and are more susceptible to disease when the hive is sited in the path of cold winds.

### Compass bearings

Field bees take their bearings from the position of the sun and usually fly from mid-morning until mid-afternoon. So it is advisable not to place hives to the north or west of buildings and to face the hive entrance to the south or southeast but not into prevailing winds.

### Valleys are preferable

If there are hillsides at a location, site any hive in the valley as the bees will then fly uphill when unladen and downhill when laden with pollen or nectar, but beware of frost pockets in the bottom of valleys. Also bear in mind the access to and from the hive with loaded supers to ease your own journeys.

### Convenience and consideration

Locate the hives near to home in order to make the necessary regular checks less laborious, time-consuming, and expensive. Hives near roads, pavements, or bridle paths can cause a nuisance to their regular users and should be avoided. It is a good plan to have a high hedge in the flight path so that inward or outward bound bees are forced to fly higher to surmount it. A hedge causes less wind turbulence than a fence or brick wall. Hives should not be positioned in straight rows facing the same way as this will

**Above:** *These hives have been arranged in a horseshoe shape, all pointing inwards, to make it easy for foraging bees to locate them.*

cause drifting of bees into other hives when returning from foraging, especially in windy conditions.

## NECTAR AND POLLEN

Field bees spend their time foraging for four basic things:

- Pollen
- Propolis
- Water
- Nectar

### Pollen

Bees visit flowers to collect pollen and nectar for food. Pollen is essential because it is the bee's only natural source of protein. Without it, colonies would be unable to produce new bees and they would eventually die out.

### Water

Honeybees also require water in addition to pollen and nectar for their survival.

### Propolis

This sticky substance from the buds of trees is used by bees to glue all cracks and close gaps of less than 3 mm.

### Nectar

This is the bait that plants produce to lure insects into pollination. It is a sickly sweet mix of sugars and water. Flowering plants provide food for honeybees; in turn, bees provide pollination for many plants, enabling them to reproduce.

Nectar is the carbohydrate portion of the bee's food and is also the raw material of honey. Bees convert nectar into honey by adding an enzyme that breaks down the complex sugars into simple sugars. During this time, bees will reduce the moisture content of the nectar to less than eighteen percent by fanning air through the hive.

## NECTAR-PRODUCING PLANTS

To produce honey successfully, you must have your honeybee colonies at peak strength when the major nectar-producing plants in your area begin to bloom. To properly manage honeybee colonies so that their populations will increase and peak at the correct time, a working knowledge is needed of the nectar- and pollen-producing plants in the vicinity of apiaries.

This knowledge determines when to stimulate brood production, add supers, use swarm control measures, harvest honey, requeen, prepare colonies for winter, and locate the most productive apiary sites. If left on their own, most honeybee colonies do not begin increasing their populations rapidly until the major nectar flow starts.

As a result, the nectar flow is usually over before the honeybee colonies are strong enough to produce a surplus of honey.

Beginners in beekeeping frequently ask questions about growing special crops or plants specifically for honey production. In general, it is not economically practical to grow a crop for the honeybees alone. Beekeepers are largely dependent on cultivated crops, which are grown for other purposes, or on wild plants.

However, under certain conditions, it may be advantageous for beekeepers to use specific nectar- and pollen-producing plants in landscaping their own land and to plant certain crops on idle land. Either case would require the selection of specific plants or crops adapted to, and suitable for, specific locations, situations and types of soil.

Nectar production and secretion will be affected by many factors, including the following:
- Fertility of the plant
- Soil moisture and acidity
- Altitude
- Latitude
- Length of day
- Number of hours of sunlight per day
- Weather.

# What do I do?

Whether you keep bees for profit or as a hobby, make sure you keep records. One good method is to keep a diary. It can be kept in a plastic bag under the roof of each hive but it is preferable to take records indoors for consultation. Enter details such as the date the colony was established, dates of inspection, honey yield, mite treatment, and other facts that will help you keep track of a particular hive. It is also useful to record any honey plants in flower to help you to schedule management practices.

## SEASONAL MANAGEMENT

The tasks of the beekeeper will vary throughout the year, depending to some extent on the season. Here is a brief guide to the management tasks that must be performed and when to do them.

## WHEN SPRING IS IN THE AIR...

Management tasks will vary from place to place and will depend on the weather conditions but the following is a guide to the early spring activities that most beekeepers will have to carry out.
■ Put the brood box to one side and clean the hive floor. A spare floor helps with this operation.
■ Check for an increase in brood area. This shows the queen is laying well. She

should have begun laying by now.
■ Check for sufficient stores. The supply should never get below 10 lb (4.5 kg). The bees can exhaust this amount in a week if no nectar is forthcoming.

### Routine inspection
The beginner will often be tempted to open the hive and just look at the bees. Although this may be interesting, it is an unnecessary disturbance of the colony. During the swarming period, which lasts from late April to the end of June, these routine inspections should be once every seven to ten days.

There are five questions you should ask yourself when opening up a hive:
**1** Has the colony got enough room – for the bees and the nectar?
**2** Is the queen present and is she laying as expected at that time of year?
**3** Is the colony expanding (in early spring) and are there queen cells (later on)?
**4** Are there any abnormalities or signs of disease?
**5** Has the colony sufficient stores until the next inspection?

Depending on the answers you get to these questions, you may or may not need to take further action. A routine examination like this need not take more than ten minutes per hive. A beginner will take longer but, with practice, this can be done quite quickly.

### Queen marking

On most inspections, you only need to see eggs in the brood area to confirm that the queen is there. However, there will be times when you actually need to find the queen. To make this task a manageable one, it is common practice to mark the queen. Do this in early spring or in late autumn when there are less bees in the hive. Special queen marking cages are available to immobilize the queen. Dab a spot on her thorax, either with some special queen-marking paint or some white correction fluid. There are five internationally recognized colors that are used to indicate the queen's age:

- Years ending zero and five are blue
- One and six are white
- Two and seven are yellow
- Three and eight are red
- Four and nine are green.

However, some white correction fluid is adequate for all years, if wished.

### Queen clipping

When about one-third of one wing of the queen is cut off with some sharp scissors, the queen is unable to fly. This will not prevent swarming but it will stop the prime swarm absconding with the old queen. This will enable the beekeeper to miss out one routine inspection during the swarming season.

**Opposite:** *Regular inspections should be carried out, especially in late spring and early summer when swarmings may occur.*

**Above:** *Queen marking is a useful practice. Use some white correction fluid as shown here.*

## AS THE BLOSSOMS BEGIN TO SHOW…

In mid-spring, you will need to do the following:

- Provide free access to the hive entrance by removing the entrance blocks and clearing any plant growth in front of the entrance, if necessary.
- If full frames of honey and pollen are next to the brood nest, blocking its expansion, rearrange the frames in the brood chamber so that a frame of empty drawn comb separates the brood from the food stores. As these frames fill with brood, provide more space by adding a super per space for the bees.

### Artificial swarming

When queen cells are found the first time, they may be destroyed and, in about twenty percent of cases, the colony may not build any more queen cells. There is no point in destroying cells the second time as the bees will continue to build more and more and will swarm in any case. You must create conditions that will stop the swarming urge in the colony. The method requires some additional empty equipment: an empty brood box with frames of foundation or drawn comb, a bottom board, and a hive cover.

To do this successfully, the queen must be found and then put with two frames of brood into the empty hive. Any queen cells on the two frames must be destroyed. The rest of the space in the brood box is filled with the empty frames. This box is placed on the original site. Any supers with honey are also placed on this box.

The rest of the frames are placed in the second box. Select one good unsealed queen cell and destroy the rest. Position this hive alongside the one that contains the queen.

All the foraging bees will return to the original site and continue with honey production. As most of the brood has been removed and few young bees are left, the swarming impulse will be stopped, at least for several weeks. The young bees in the other brood box will raise a new queen and build up.

If this operation is done with an unsealed queen cell, then you must move the hive after seven days to the other side of the one containing the queen. This move will milk off some more foraging

## SMOKING BEES

Bees communicate extensively by smell and the queen secretes pheromones, which trigger much of what happens in the dark interior of the hive. To gain some measure of control, beekeepers have developed the practice of smoking, which entails the puffing of cool, white smoke into the hive.

For reasons not clearly understood, smoke stimulates bees to move to honey stores and engorge on honey, diverting their attention sufficiently to enable the beekeeper to accomplish management tasks. This can clearly be seen after applying smoke to a colony. Early smokers were little more than a smouldering fire beneath or near a hive. Later, tobacco pipes were modified to direct smoke into hives as were other early devices.

Smoker fuels are as numerous as are the beekeepers who use them. However, common fuels include grass clippings, rotten wood, wood shavings, and burlap. Anything can be used that produces cool, white billowing smoke just so long as it has not been treated with pesticides or fire retardant. Under normal conditions, smoke is effective for about four minutes, but it needs to be skillfully applied as required to keep the colony under control.

**Right:** Dried grass, leaves, or small pieces of rotten wood are pushed down into the smoker before lighting.

**Below:** When a cool, white billowing smoke is obtained, it can be puffed into the hive so that the beekeeper can work unhindered by the bees in the colony inside.

**Above:** *The foraging bees return to the hive and enter through a very narrow entrance. This can be blocked to exclude wasps.*

bees and reinforce the original colony so that honey production will not suffer. If only sealed queen cells are available, the second move cannot be done as the young queen will be ready to go on a mating flight.

At some stage the old queen can be killed and the colonies united, or both colonies can be maintained to increase the number of hives. If the artificial swarming is done early in the season, the second colony will be able to produce a super of honey.

### Collecting swarms

Even with the best management, there will be the odd occasion when a swarm will issue from a colony. Beekeepers must be prepared to collect their own swarms and, as a public duty, also collect any other swarms in their locality.

When the swarm has settled on a low branch of a tree or bush, it is easy to place a container, such as a cardboard box

sitting on a cloth, beneath the cluster and then give the branch a hard shake. The bees will fall into the box and you can invert the box on to the cloth.

Leave a small opening at the base so that bees can get in and leave the box until the evening. Just before sunset, all the bees will be inside the box. Cover the box with the cloth, tie with some string, and remove it.

If the swarm is higher up a tree, you will need some steps or a ladder. Very occasionally, a swarm may be so high that it's impossible to get to it. At times, swarms will settle on things such as fence posts. In this situation, place the inverted container over the swarm and smoke the bees, making them move up. If a swarm is found on something solid like a wall, the best tools are a dustpan and brush.

If the swarm is from an unknown origin, after putting it into an empty hive, use an approved mite treatment. As there is no brood, all varroa mites will be destroyed. If the swarm is placed in a hive that contains mostly, or all, frames with foundation, feed the bees with 8 pints (4.5 liters) of sugar syrup. Delay feeding strange swarms for two days. By this time, the bees will have used up all the honey they carried with them and also any diseases that are carried with the honey.

You should collect any swarms that emerge from your own colony and rehouse them in a new hive placed on the original site. Move the original hive and destroy all but one queen cell.

## WHEN THE NECTAR FLOWS FREELY...

In summer, at the end of the fruit bloom to the beginning of the main nectar flow, you should do the following:

■ Watch for signs of swarming. You should practice some form of swarm control and prevention.

■ Maintain supering for honey production.

## WHEN THE LEAVES BEGIN TO FALL...

There are more seasonal jobs to be carried out in autumn:

■ Check that the cluster contains bees, to cover five to twelve frames.

■ Unite small colonies with stronger ones.

■ Feed the colony fumagillin-treated syrup if Nosema disease is in your area. This disease can reduce the cluster size such that it will die of freezing.

■ If the colony does not have about 50 lb (23 kg) honey, feed sugar syrup to make up the shortage. Do this in September. Insert entrance blocks before feeding.

■ Build a windbreak for protection.

■ Put mouse guards on the entrances.

■ Apply an approved treatment for varroa mites.

## YEAR AROUND...

If your bees are located in a rural area where there are also bears, you may need to protect the hives from bear damage.

Encircle the hives with an electrified fence or a fence strong enough to deter bears.

## AT THE SEASON'S END...

■ The main thing to check in winter is that the hives are not damaged by animals or storms.

■ If you provide the proper conditions in the autumn, there is no reason to open the hive in winter. Opening it up unnecessarily only creates problems.

**Above:** *By opening the hive, the beekeeper can check the sealed brood cells.*

# What to expect

## BEE TALK

The language of bees does not have an alphabet or words, but the work of Professor Karl von Frisch has enabled us to interpret something of their communication system. His experiments clearly show that the bees have an accurate language based on characteristic dances, odor, and taste perception.

### Language dances

When a field bee locates a source of pollen or nectar, she can communicate this information to other bees in the colony accurately as to direction, distance from the hive, and a sample of the nectar from the plants supplying it. The language dance performed within a colony is orientated on the combs in relation to the sun. The angle between the sun, food source, and hive determines the direction of the dance.

■ A dance straight up on the comb's vertical axis means toward the sun.

■ A dance to the right, so many degrees to the right of the sun.

■ A dance to the left, so many degrees to the left of the sun.

■ A rapid dance means a short distance.

■ A slower dance means an increased distance.

The bees do not actually have to see the sun to be capable of transmitting or interpreting this food source information,

since they can perceive and interpret direction from the polarized light they receive from the sky. The plant producing the food is identified by the odor association of the food gathered by the dancing bee. Dances similar to those giving directions for food are also performed by scout bees that find a suitable new location for a swarm that has issued from a colony.

## SWARMING

Unexpected swarming can be the beekeeper's nightmare but it is nature's way of replicating the colony and must be accepted as one of the challenges of honeybee management. Think of it as a pan of simmering water on a stove: too much heat and it boils over; too little heat and it remains lukewarm. The beekeeper wants to keep the bees simmering away nicely rather than boiling up or turning lukewarm to the task of honey production.

### Preparing to swarm

When preparing themselves to swarm, bees build a large number of queen cells along the bottom of the comb and, shortly before a fresh queen emerges, the queen stops laying and field work ceases. The swarm bees (usually at least half of the colony) gorge themselves on honey and

leave the hive with the old queen, flying a short distance to hang together in a dense ball-like formation from a nearby tree or bush.

Here they await signs of possible new living quarters from the scout bees and during this interim they are at their most docile and can be handled without undue fear of stinging. However, as soon as a destination is decided upon, the bees break out into a clamorous cloud of rowdy activity, intent on reaching their new home, albeit an empty hive or a hollow tree.

### Why bees swarm

The instinct to swarm is triggered partly by nature and partly by the quality of life inside the hive. The following points are worth bearing in mind.

▨ Overcrowding is the commonest cause and cramped conditions can themselves be worsened by a lack of supers.

▨ The hive can become congested when springtime pollen abundance triggers a

**Above:** *Bees seem to have developed their own language within the darkened hive.*

quick increase in rearing activities. Brood cells are filled faster than they are emptied by the emergence of new bees and therefore the area given over to the nursery balloons in size. There is also a commensurate expansion of the areas devoted to storing nectar and pollen. If space is not freed to accommodate all this growth, then the urge to swarm will build.

▨ Spring is an important time to inspect the colony to ensure the provision of ample space for brood rearing and also for honey storage.

▨ When the nectar flow inaugurates, honey supers will need adding and checks should start for signs of swarming. First intimations will be queen cells placed along the bottoms of frames. There are several recognized ways to deal with the colony at this stage to prevent a swarm issuing from the hive.

## PESTS AND HEALTH PROBLEMS

Bees are vulnerable to a variety of pests and potential health problems and you should be ever vigilant to detect any early warning signs and also to prevent some of these occurring if possible. Diseases can be divided into two groups:
- Those of the adult bees
- Those of the brood.

Therefore it is most important that the beginner in beekeeping skills learns to recognize what healthy brood looks like.

### Nosema

This disease is caused by the protozoan *Nosema apis*, which attacks the true stomach and intestines of adult bees. It is widespread and especially troublesome in colder areas where winter is long with only a few flight days. The disease can be associated with diarrhea in winter. If the colony fails to build up in the spring, then Nosema is often the cause. Positive identification can be done only by microscopic examination; cure and prevention can be brought about by feeding the bees with medicated syrup.

### Varroa mite

*Varroa jacobsoni* is one of the most serious pests of the honeybee. It is a parasite that attacks both brood and adults. Unless special measures are taken to search for the mite, early detection is unlikely. The mites develop in sealed brood cells. Heavy infestation of several mites per cell can produce deformed bees.

- Adult female mites are reddish-brown to dark brown, oval and flattened in shape, approximately one-twenty-fifth of an inch long, and they can be seen easily with the unaided eye.
- Adult male Varroa mites are much smaller and lighter. They are only found in the sealed cells.

Female mites enter honeybee brood cells shortly before the cells are capped, feed on the larvae, and lay eggs. Adult mites develop in six to ten days and mate in the cells before emerging with the bee. Male mites die soon after mating. During spring and summer, most mites are found in the sealed brood cells (especially drone brood). In late autumn and winter, most mites are found on the adult workers as there is no brood at that time.

### Treating infested colonies

Unchecked infestations can kill colonies in less than three years. Colonies infested with varroa mites can be treated by means of an approved mite treatment, available from most beekeeping supply distributors. After removing the honey supers in the autumn, place the strips in the brood area of the hive, according to the manufacturer's instructions.

**Note:** The bee louse resembles the varroa mite in size and color. However, the bee louse is a wingless insect with six legs that extend to the side. The varroa mite has eight legs that extend forward. The bee louse rarely builds up high enough to cause significant problems but it can leave traces under sealed frames of honey.

### Brood diseases

American foul brood (AFB) and European foul brood (EFB) can be spread by bees robbing dead colonies and by the beekeeper manipulating hives. Most state departments of agriculture provide colony inspection services to help deter the spread. They also provide descriptive literature and treatment recommendations.

It is strongly recommended that, as a new beekeeper, you join your local beekeeping association and work with more experienced beekeepers to learn how to identify and deal with all bee diseases.

## OTHER PESTS

### Wax moths

These enter hives where they can cause damage if the colony is not strong enough to protect the comb or too many empty supers are on the hive. Wax moths also damage any unprotected combs in storage. When bee colonies are bothered by wax moths or other insect pests, such as wasps or ants, it usually means that the colony is weak. Building up colony strength allows the bees to repel them. To prevent wax moth damage to stored equipment, use PDB crystals from equipment suppliers.

### Small hive beetles

This pest was first identified in the United States in 1998. Like wax moths, the beetles attack colonies that are weak and have more comb than they can protect. Treatments are being developed; consult with your local beekeeping association.

### Mice

These might nest in combs in winter storage. They also enter hives in the late autumn to build their nests. Honeybee colonies can be protected by placing special mouse guards across the entrance. These do not hamper the movement of bees in and out of the hive.

### Bee poisoning

Pesticide poisoning can come from farm crops or from amateur gardeners in towns. The best rule of thumb is to establish and maintain communication with nearby farmers so that you will be notified before pesticide applications. The key to protecting bee colonies is always prevention, which is usually possible through cooperation between the beekeeper and those people who might apply pesticides.

# What do I get?

## HONEY

Honey is a concentrated solution of two sugars, glucose and fructose, with small amounts of at least twenty-two other more complex sugars. Many other substances also occur in honey but the sugars are the major components.

The principal physical characteristics and behavior of honey are due to its sugars, but the minor constituents, pigments, acids, and minerals, are largely responsible for the differences in taste and color of honey.

As found in the hive, honey is a remarkable material, having been ripened by bees from the thin, easily spoiled, sweet liquid nectar into a stable, high-density, high-energy food.

It displays a rich kaleidoscope of color, passing from very pale yellow through amber to a darkish red-amber to nearly black. The variations are entirely due to the plant source of the honey.

The flavor and aroma of honey vary even more than its color. Although there is a characteristic honey flavor, almost an infinite number of aroma and flavor variations can exist. As with color, the variations appear to be governed by the floral source. In general, light-colored honey is mild in flavor whereas a darker honey has a more pronounced taste.

## HONEY'S MEDICINAL USES

An ancient medicinal use for honey was as a dressing for wounds and inflammations. Today, medicinal uses of honey are largely confined to folk medicine. On the other hand, since milk can be a carrier of some diseases, it was once thought that honey might likewise be such a carrier. Some years ago this idea was examined by adding nine common pathogenic bacteria to honey. All the bacteria died within a few hours or days. Honey is not a suitable medium for bacteria for two reasons: it is fairly acid and it is too high in sugar content for growth to occur. This killing of bacteria by high sugar content is called the osmotic effect. It seems to function by drying out the bacteria. Some bacteria, however, can survive in the resting spore form but do not grow in honey. When used as a wound dressing, honey produces hydrogen peroxide as it gets diluted by body fluids.

**Above:** *A remarkable range of products can be obtained, including honey, beeswax candles, wood polish, and moisturizing creams.*

## Water content

The natural moisture of honey in the comb is that remaining from the nectar after ripening. After extraction of the honey, its moisture content may change, depending on the conditions of storage. It is one of honey's most important characteristics and will influence the keeping quality.

Beekeepers, as well as honey buyers, know that the water content of honey varies greatly, ranging from fifteen to twenty-one percent. If honey has more than nineteen percent moisture and contains a sufficient number of yeast spores, it will ferment. When extracting honey, ensure that the combs are capped with wax. Bees will cap honey only if the water content is below the critical point.

## Food value and granulation

Honey is primarily a high-energy carbohydrate food with its distinct flavors that cannot be found elsewhere. The honey sugars are largely the easily digestible simple sugars, similar to those in many fruits. Honey can be regarded as a good health food. Most honey will eventually granulate, or crystallize. The rapidity of granulation depends on the ratio of glucose and levulose. Some honeys, such as tupelo and sage, may be stored for years without granulation. Other honey must be extracted immediately or it will granulate in the comb.

## Honey extraction

Removing honey from the comb is not easy since there is no simple, neat and inexpensive way of doing it. It is very important that all utensils and containers, stainless steel or plastic, and other items that come in contact with the honey must be kept clean during the operation. The first step is the removal of wax cappings.

## How to remove wax cappings

Combs of honey should be uncapped on both sides. A thin layer of wax and honey is cut from the surface of each comb with a back-and-forth sawing movement, as the knife is held against the top and bottom bars of the frame.

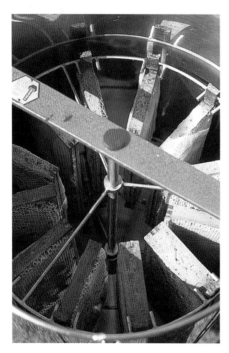

**1** First uncap one side, then turn the frame and uncap the other side. The frame is best held by pivoting the end bar on a point of a nail that is supported by a strip of wood lying across the top of the container that receives the cappings.
**2** Hold the frame at an angle, so the cappings fall free of the comb into the container below.
**3** Or use a special uncapping fork instead of a knife. By using this method, less honey is removed with the cappings.

## Separating the honey from the wax

Since the cappings contain a large amount of honey after they are cut from the combs, it is important to have some way of separating the honey from the wax. Allow the cappings to drain in a stainless steel or plastic container with a screen at the base.

## Extractors that produce liquid honey

To produce liquid honey, you need an extractor that uses centrifugal force to spin the honey from the cells. Various types and sizes are manufactured commercially.

The small-scale beekeeper often uses a two- or four-frame basket extractor. The uncapped combs are placed vertically in the baskets that support them.

Either the hand- or power-driven baskets are turned slowly at first. If the

**Left:** *To extract the honey from the frames, they are placed vertically in an extractor and are then spun. Nowadays, most extractors are power-operated rather than manually driven.*

extractor is turned too rapidly, the weight of the honey will break the combs. The combs are spun until about half of the honey is removed from the first side. Then the combs are reversed and spun until the second side is completely extracted.

Finally, the combs are reversed a second time and the remaining honey is removed. These are tangental extractors.

In the radial type of extractor, the combs are placed like the spokes of a wheel and both sides are extracted at the same time. These extractors are normally power-operated. The time required to throw honey from the combs depends on the density and temperature of the honey. Watch the side of the tank to see when the honey stops flowing from the combs.

### Straining the honey

After the honey is extracted, it contains air bubbles, pollen, and pieces of wax. Excessive pollen, can be avoided by keeping brood combs out of the honey supers. Strain the honey through a plastic or stainless steel sieve to remove most foreign matter and leave it to settle in plastic buckets. Any remaining small particles will rise to the top and can be removed later. If wished, honey can be filtered through a fine nylon mesh, but it will have to heated slightly to do this.

Bulk containers for storing honey should have airtight lids. Honey should never be left exposed to the open air as it will absorb moisture from the air and cause fermentation.

### DID YOU KNOW?

The term "honeymoon" is associated with the ancient custom of drinking honey-based mead for a "moon" (month) after marriage in the hope of producing a male child.

### Granulated honey

Granulation is a natural process in which the sugars in honey crystallize out to a solid. The floral source and storage conditions can affect the rate of crystallization. Storage at 50–55°F (10–13°C) will promote granulation. To reliquefy granulated honey in containers, place the container in a warm place or set in a warm pan of water. Avoid direct heat, which will scorch the honey.

## BEESWAX

If you keep bees, you can expect to get beeswax, which is a very useful substance and has many different uses.

### Lubrication

■ Use beeswax on nails and screws to make them drive more easily.

■ Apply to sticking drawers, doors, and windows to lessen friction.

■ Apply to needles and thread for easier penetration of heavy material.

## Metal preservation

■ Screws, nails or metal parts will not rust readily if they are immersed in molten beeswax and left until the temperature of the metal reaches that of the molten wax. The metal will absorb some of the wax and become rust resistant. For this to work, it is important for the metal to remain in the molten wax long enough to attain the proper temperature. Otherwise there will be only a surface coating of wax which will quickly wear.

## Metal polish

■ To make a protective coating and polish for metal, mix turpentine (8 parts), beeswax (1 part), and boiled linseed oil (½ part).
■ This mixture also makes a good lubricant for saw blades and sawbench surfaces.

## Wood polish

■ There are differing proportions of beeswax and boiled linseed oil and/or turpentine that make a good polish. It may take some experimentation to find the appropriate consistency, but to make a paste, mix 1 part beeswax to 2 parts turpentine, and 2 parts linseed oil. The larger the proportion of beeswax, the stiffer the final product.

## Leather treatment.

■ To make a conditioner and waterproofing for leather, combine equal parts of beeswax, tallow, and neatsfoot oil. Before applying, warm the mixture slightly and have the leather at room temperature or higher.

## Candles

■ Candles made from pure beeswax are superior to those made from paraffin wax in that they burn longer, smell pleasant, and are virtually drip-free when made from well-cleaned beeswax.
■ To make good candles it is also important to use proper beeswax candle wicking of the correct size, not just string.
■ As a guide to making candles, three pairs of 10-in (25-cm) molded or dipped table candles can be made per 1 lb (450 g) wax.
**Note:** Beeswax should always be melted in a double boiler arrangement for safety. It is highly flammable in contact with direct heat. When other ingredients are to be added, they may be added cold and then everything should be heated together, or pre-warmed materials may be added to molten wax. Beeswax melts at approximately 147°F (60°C).

## NEXT STEPS

Join the local beekeeping association. This will bring you in contact with other beekeepers who will be able to help if needed, and will offer advice. There will also be apiary meetings, honey shows in the summer, and lectures in the winter. The association may have a library of beekeeping books and honey extractors that can be hired for a small charge. To locate beekeepers in your area, contact your county's agricultural extension office; it may be listed under the name of your state agricultural university.

# Further reading

*ABC & XYZ of Bee Culture:
An Encyclopedia of
Beekeeping,* edited by Roger
Morse & Kim Flottum (A.I.
Root), 1990.
*The Hive and the Honey Bee,*
Joe Graham (Dadant &
Sons), 1992.

*Raising Milk Goats the
Modern Way,* Jerry Belanger
(Storey Books), 1990.
*Raising Poultry the Modern
Way,* Leonard S. Mercia
and Kimberly Foster
(Storey Books), 1990.

# Useful addresses

**American Beekeeping
Federation**
P.O. Box 1038
Jesup, GA 31598

**National Honey Board**
390 Lashley St.
Longmont, CO 80501

For beekeeping contacts in
every state, access the
website
<http://bee.airoot.com/
beeculture/who.html>

**American Dairy Goat
Association**
P.O. Box 865
Spindale, NC 28160
(704) 286-3801
www.adga.org

**American Poultry
Association**
133 Milville St.
Mendon, MA 01756
(508) 473-8769

**U.S. Poultry & Egg
Association**
www.poultryegg.org

**International Waterfowl
Breeders Association**
http://users.isaac.net/
gamefarm/wfoul.html

# Index

## Acknowledgments

The publishers would like to thank the following for their help in compiling the book: Joe Coxey, The Priory Waterfowl Farm, Ixworth, Bury St. Edmunds, Suffolk

Steven Florey, The Henhouse, Thorndon, Suffolk Also David Barker, Jacqui and Roger Collier, Peter Cox, Mrs. Devenish, Julie Lovett, Jenny Mann, and Jean and Zig Ruskin